The British and Russian royal families had just three full meetings before the Romanovs' tragic end in 1918. In *The Imperial Tea Party*, Frances Welch draws back the curtain on those fraught encounters, which had far-reaching consequences for 20th-century Europe and beyond.

Russia and Britain were never natural bedfellows. But the marriage, in 1894, of Queen Victoria's favourite granddaughter, Alicky, to the Tsarevich Nicholas marked the beginning of an uneasy Anglo-Russian entente that would last until the Russian Revolution of 1917.

The three extraordinary meetings that took place during those years, although generally hailed as successes, were beset by misunderstandings and misfortunes. The Tsar and Tsarina complained bitterly about the weather when staying at Balmoral, while British courtiers later criticised the Russians' hospitality, from the food to the music to the slow service.

In this wonderfully sharp account, Frances Welch presents a vivid snapshot of two dynasties at a time of social unrest. The families could not know, as they waved each other fond goodbyes from their boats at Cowes in 1909, that they would

THE IMPERIAL TEA PARTY

FRANCES WELCH

The following photographs are reproduced with the kind permission of Ian Shapiro: front cover image (repeated on page 81) and pages 41, 64, 85, 123, 145, 177, 193 and 224.

Ian Shapiro also kindly lent the postcard of the Tsar's arrival at Balmoral (p33); the Tsar's letter to General Gardiner (p61); the Balmoral seating plan (p69); the menu for Queen Victoria's celebration dinner (p79); the menu from the Victoria and Albert yacht (p160); the Izvolsky letters (p201); the silver cigarette case gifted by the Tsarina (p229).

First published in 2018 by Short Books,
Unit 316, ScreenWorks, 22 Highbury Grove,
London, N5 2ER

This paperback edition published in 2019

10 9 8 7 6 5 4 3 2 1

A CIP catalogue record for this book is
available from the British Library.

ISBN: 978-1-78072-392-1

Cover design by Two Associates

Printed at CPI Group (UK) Ltd, Croydon, CR0 4YY

For Florence, Grace and JJ.

"Man's sensitivity to little things and insensitivity to the greatest are the signs of a strange disorder."

Pascal, *Pensées*

"Fate is not an eagle, it creeps like a rat."

Elizabeth Bowen, *The House In Paris*, 1938

BALMORAL

On Friday, 11th September 1896, the young Tsarina of Russia wrote a buoyant telegram to her 77-year-old grandmother, Queen Victoria. The pair were to be reunited, at Balmoral, after being parted for more than two years: 'Fondest thanks dear letter Nicky agrees to all sends much love fine weather Alix.'

The 24-year-old Tsarina was due to travel from Denmark in just over a week. The imperial couple had not visited Britain since their marriage in 1894 and the recent coronation of Alix's husband, Nicky. The Queen would be seeing the imperial couple's ten-month baby daughter, Olga, for the first time.

The close attachment between Alix and her grandmother had been forged over idyllic summers at various royal residences. Alix, or 'Alicky', as her grandmother called her, had developed a particular fondness for Balmoral. At the Russian court, the Tsarina had maintained her happy memories with a life-size portrait of Victoria, chintzes from the Maples catalogue and British foodstuffs. As the Tsar's younger sister Olga reported: 'Nicky once complained Alix kept him awake by crunching her favourite English biscuits.'

A week later, the Queen received another telegram, altering the date of her granddaughter's arrival: 'Nicky and Alicky much distressed that on account of new ship will not be able to start till Sunday arriving 22nd hope you won't mind Old Alix.' The 'new ship' was the 4,500-ton imperial yacht, swiftly referred to by her husband as the 'marvellous *Standart*'.

But the punctilious Queen did mind, complaining of 'great inconvenience'. The equerry-in-waiting, the Hon William Carington, was obliged to reassure her: 'All arrangements exactly the same but Tuesday not Monday'. The Aberdeenshire Constabulary, however, remained in a muddle. The Chief Constable's office issued an elaborately inscribed report marred by ugly crossings out, with Tuesday and 22nd mysteriously erased and Monday and 21st scrawled on top.

There may have been further complications caused by the fact that the Tsar, and presumably his suite, stuck resolutely to the Julian calendar, which was then 12 days behind the Gregorian calendar used by the British. As far as the Tsar was concerned, the arrival date had changed from the 9th to the 10th of September.

Alix's breezy 'Nicky agrees to all' in the first telegram appeared increasingly wide of the mark, as the Tsar's naval attaché now began a huffy exchange of telegrams with the beleaguered equerry. While taking the alteration of the date in his stride, Carington had not been so happy to receive last-minute quibbles about landing docks. He immediately telegraphed the Queen's private secretary, Sir Arthur Bigge: 'Russian embassy says Tsar wants to land North Queen's ferry and not Leith.' He complained that the Prince of Wales (later Edward VII) himself had been obliged to weigh in, sending his own sharp telegram to the attaché: 'deprecating changing Leith for North Queen's ferry'.

At one point Carington seemed to soften in his attitude

to the bumptious Russian attaché, with a light-hearted instruction to Bigge to overlook the dock debacle. Worried that his adversary might 'get into a row', he wrote: 'He was very excited at first but is now settling down and making himself very useful.' He added wryly: 'If anything goes wrong I conclude he will be sent to Siberia.'

But, three days later, the pair were again at loggerheads, with an outburst from Carington: 'The Russian naval attaché has just proposed that the plan of the steamers for disembarkation should be set aside in favour of the yacht coming into Leith Harbour,' he fumed. 'As this is the third change of great magnitude he has proposed, I was constrained to tell him that, unless I receive the Emperor's commands in writing to that effect, I could not undertake at this late hour so important an alteration.'

Carington's exasperation increased as the Russians' demands for changes were matched by a refusal to provide any detailed information. He complained to Bigge that he was no further with his inquiries about luggage: 'We have received no answer to that question or, between you and me, to any other addressed to that quarter.'

Two days before their arrival, on 20th September, the Tsarina wrote her third and most cheery telegram to the Queen: 'Just leaving beautiful Sunday weather so happy meeting soon many kisses.' Her repeated references to fine weather would later strike a particularly jarring note. At the beginning of September, Sir Francis Knollys, private secretary to the Prince of Wales, had sent an optimistic message to Bigge regarding the likely temperature in Scotland: 'Take care to acquaint the Emperor that it will be warm.'

In fact, the imperial couple would be greeted at Leith by

conditions described by *The Scotsman* newspaper as 'dreich and misty with driving rain'. And, as it turned out, the weather barely improved throughout the imperial couple's 11 days at Balmoral. The Queen's harrowing descriptions included: 'threatening', 'frosty' and, on one especially bad day, 'terrible pouring wet morning, with much darkness'.

While the royal parties fretted about rain, the authorities grappled with unprecedented security arrangements. The British and Russian royal families had close blood ties – Nicky and Alicky were both first cousins of 'Georgie', the future George V – and for much of the sentimental British public, a Romanov visit would have been cause for celebration. However, among radical left-wing factions, Nicky was merely the latest in a long line of autocrats, with a poor record on civil liberties and censorship.

In an era of letters and telegrams, keeping ahead of potential troublemakers was an enormous challenge. Courtiers liaised with the Metropolitan Police and the Aberdeenshire constabulary; the constabulary, in turn, were in daily contact with continental police. Hundreds of plain-clothes policemen would work alongside 24 constables and four sergeants from the Metropolitan Police. The movements of the Tsar's secret police, the *okhrana*, however, remained a mystery; clues seldom went beyond rumours of bodyguards secreting themselves behind bushes, armed with spyglasses. One metropolitan police report later revealed slightly more detail: '3 Russian detective officers present now residing with... head gardener to Her Majesty the Queen'. But on 8th September, Carington was still writing coy notes to Bigge: 'From a remark I heard dropped at the Russian embassy I fancy the two persons who are to live in the artists rooms at Balmoral are Russian Police.'

Railway workers would patrol the track covering the Romanovs' proposed train route from Leith to Ballater (the closest station to Balmoral). Bridges and viaducts would be supervised by local police, while a pilot engine ran ahead of the trains. One newspaper reassured readers that there was a 'staff of telegraph linesmen and operators with appliances for effecting telegraphic communication'. The Aberdeenshire constabulary promised that its constables would be vigilant: 'They will see that a sharp look-out is kept for suspicious strangers.'

The Times insisted finally: 'Every precaution has been and will be taken which human foresight can compass to ensure a safe and speedy arrival... on no previous occasion have such elaborate preparations been made for the reception of royalty as at present, while the precautions taken to secure the safety of the imperial visitors were extremely thorough and minute.'

Sir Edward Bradford, commissioner of the Metropolitan Police, agreed, assuring Bigge: 'The Emperor is safer here than anywhere else in the world and you can assure the Queen and all concerned. It is a great happiness to be able to feel this and to have no hesitation in saying it.'

Days before the Romanovs' arrival, however, tensions rose as Scotland Yard released confusing information about a plan to attack the imperial family. Reports appeared of the so-called 'dynamite conspiracy', featuring plans by Irish-American activists and Russian nihilists to bomb one of the trains. The ringleader, it was reported, held a forged letter for the Tsar saying he was an envoy of the Queen. It emerged that a cache of dynamite had, indeed, been found in an anarchists' basement in Antwerp and three arrests had been made. But there had never been any plan to assassinate the Tsar.

While Carington was sorting out the dock debacle, Bigge was receiving reassuring notes from the assistant commissioner of the Metropolitan Police. The assistant commissioner, Robert Anderson, was adamant that the recent plot: 'did not aim at any personal injury either to the Queen or the Tsar; moreover the gang is now broken up and the practical danger which was serious and urgent is happily at an end'. In several follow-up letters, Anderson carried on protesting that he himself had never spoken to the press. He wrote with such vehemence that he feared, finally, that he was coming across as 'egotistical'.

Sir Matthew Ridley, of the home department, wrote to Bigge, echoing Anderson: 'I have been watching the operation of these ruffians… I do not believe that this plot had anything to do with the Tsar's visit.'

It was widely mooted that, on this occasion, the British press had allowed itself to be carried away. A Boston newspaper ran the headline: 'All England terrified. The London press suddenly becomes sensational… if printers' ink could produce a panic, London would be in a state of nervous prostration.'

But *The Scotsman* newspaper gave a sober description of the resulting unease: 'The rumours and suspicions of a plot against their [the Romanovs'] lives… were enough to create a certain feeling of anxiety in the minds of the public of the country. That harm should have befallen them anywhere would have been a mournful calamity; that it should have reached them in Scotland would have been an unspeakable grief to the nation.'

Queen Victoria's mounting excitement at the prospect of her reunion with Alix and her introduction to baby Olga may well have been tempered by worries about the family's safety. She had never been under any illusions about the dangers her favourite granddaughter would face when she married the young Russian Tsarevich. Civil unrest was endemic in Russia: Nicky's grandfather, Tsar Alexander II, had been assassinated just 15 years previously.

Nicky's coronation, four months before, had been dogged by chaos and tragedy. During a presentation of commemorative gifts at the Khodynka Fields, in Moscow, there had been a crowd surge during which nearly 1,500 people were crushed to death. That night, Nicky had made one of his first deeply unpopular decisions as tsar: to attend a party at the French embassy. He had been reluctant to go, but had been swayed by his domineering uncles. He was to develop a reputation for being easily led; a weakness which would colour his 21-year-reign.

At the time of the couple's engagement, the Queen had written a prescient letter to her eldest daughter, Vicky: 'The state of Russia is so bad, so rotten, that at any moment something dreadful might happen… the wife of the heir to the throne is in a difficult and precarious position.' She wrote to Alix's sister, Victoria, of her own anguish: 'the awful insecurity to which that sweet child will be exposed. I will try and bear it... my blood runs cold when I think of her so young... her dear life and above all her husband's constantly threatened and unable to see her but rarely.... Oh, how I wish it was not to be that I should lose my sweet Alicky.'

Her granddaughter had tried to dispel some of her worries, cheerily pointing out that Russia was just three days away. 'Please do not think that my marrying will make a difference in my love to you, CERTAINLY IT WILL NOT, and when I am far away, I shall long to think that there is one, the dearest and kindest woman alive, who loves me a little bit.'

How much was the anxious Queen consoled by the idea that her granddaughter's marriage might help British and Russian relations? She certainly recorded an encouraging comment from the Prime Minister at the time, Lord Rosebery: 'He spoke first of Alicky's engagement, which he felt sure must tend to peace.'

Two years on, in 1896, she seemed almost too keen to take advantage of the Russian connection. With all her excitement and worry about the visit, it soon became clear that one of her main concerns was securing the young Tsar's support for British causes abroad. Her efforts would not be appreciated by the peaceable Nicky, who was horrified to find himself endlessly embroiled in weighty discussions at Balmoral, not least two gruelling sessions with the Prime Minister, Lord Salisbury. As a doting husband of just 22 months, he wrote wistfully to his mother: 'I see even less of Alix here than at home, where deputations and audiences with ministers interfere enough.'

There was certainly room for improvement in the relations between the two countries. The British government was aware that grievances dating back to the Crimean War of the 1850s were festering, alongside the ongoing concerns about Russia's repressive regimes. The Metropolitan Police's Robert Anderson was relieved that the young Romanovs' visit was to take place at Balmoral: 'I confess a good deal has come to my knowledge which makes me glad that the Tsar is there [at Balmoral] not in London. I should be very anxious indeed if he were here.'

London had long been a magnet for Russian revolutionaries, not least because of its reputation for being lax on surveillance. Prince Pyotr Kropotkin, the founder of the anarchist newspaper *Freedom*, had arrived in Hull, in June 1876, after escaping from the Peter and Paul Fortress in St Petersburg. He described himself as overwhelmed with relief when he saw the Union Jack, 'under which so many Russian, Italian French and Hungarian refugees have found asylum'. The Prince eventually settled in Bromley.

Kropotkin would be joining his fellow Russian radical, Mikhail Bakunin, founder of the International Anarchist Movement, who had settled in Paddington Green. Bakunin, in turn, was already fraternising with the founder of communism, Karl Marx, of Kentish Town.

Joseph Conrad's novel, *The Secret Agent*, was set in London just ten years before the Balmoral visit, in 1886. The hero's foreign embassy contact makes direct reference to Britain's lax security. Conrad's group of anarchists produces a pamphlet called 'The Future of the Proletariat'. The fictional Michaelis, a prominent member of the group, is an amalgam of two real anarchists: he expounds the views of Kropotkin while sharing Bakunin's physical attributes. Michaelis and Bakunin were both, for instance, excessively large. Conrad writes that Michaelis: 'had come out of a highly hygienic prison round like a tub… as though for 15 years the servants of an outraged society had made a point of stuffing him with fattening foods in a damp and lightless cellar'.

Two years after the Balmoral visit, in 1898, a further Russian anarchist, Vladimir Burtsev, would be arrested in the British Museum Reading Room after advocating the killing of the Tsar in his magazine *Norodnaya Volya* (*The People's Will*). Like Kropotkin, Burtsev had been imprisoned in the Peter and Paul Fortress, before escaping during his subsequent exile. The prosecution had demanded Burtsev receive ten years' hard labour; he was given 18 months in jail. The police filled the public gallery to prevent Burtsev's anarchist supporters from attending the trial. Among those who succeeded in getting a seat, however, was the distinctive looking, extravagantly bearded Kropotkin.

The man put in charge of security for the Romanovs' visit was the first head of Scotland Yard's special branch, Chief Inspector William Melville. Melville had already made a name for himself, raiding anarchists' clubs and underground printing presses. A notice from the Metropolitan Police read: 'Melville and another officer will accompany Tsar from Leith to Ballater. Another London detective will be at Ballater. Three officers will remain during visit.' Melville, who later worked with the Russian secret service, would clearly not be wasting his time in Scotland, despite his sniffy complaints about: 'playing host to the Russian Security services'.

The extravagantly bearded Kropotkin

While the main focus was on security, the courtiers faced further challenges, not least finding accommodation for the large Russian contingent. Servants would have to be billeted out at local farmhouses and inns; there would be problems with communication as guests and hosts struggled with the twin hazards of the Russian language and Scottish accents. A village of stone huts, resembling grain storehouses, had to be specially constructed to help with an overspill. The scrum was such that four laundry maids were, at one point, obliged to share a single bed. Bigge referred drily to: 'The Russian occupation of Balmoral'.

Tuesday 22 September

Queen Victoria's diary: 'A pouring wet day, the worst we have had yet.'

On the day of the arrival, Queen Victoria was avidly tracking her granddaughter's movements: 'Heard on getting up that the imperial yacht was in sight of Leith'.

The shy young imperial couple had already endured weeks of ceremony and protocol, with visits to Austria, the Ukraine, Germany and Denmark. Social pressures had been exacerbated by time change issues as the couple stayed in Vienna with Emperor Franz Joseph, who rose at 4am, dined at 5pm and retired at 7pm. The mood would not have been improved by the rumour that two men had died on a mountainside, while picking bunches of edelweiss for a state banquet at the Hofburg Palace.

The couple's visit to Germany had been only a partial success. *The Times* reported that the Germans claimed the Tsarina as their own. In fact, Alix's inability to disassociate herself from her native Hesse would prove a mixed blessing. The devotion she developed for her adopted country was never fully recognised and, years later, when Russia was at war with Germany, the Tsarina was continually labelled 'Nemetz' (German).

The Tsar had not proven so popular. The Ambassador in Berlin, Frank Lascelles, wrote to the Prime Minister, Lord Salisbury: 'I see by the newspapers that the brevity of the Emperor of Russia's speeches and the fact of his having spoken in French has been somewhat criticised.' One of Lascelles' own gripes was that the Tsar overdid the presentations. He referred to the: 'enormous number of decorations which the Emperor of Russia conferred'.

The Romanovs were at Breslau station when the Russian Foreign Minister, Prince Alexei Lobanov-Rostovsky, died of apoplexy. The news of the tricky minister's demise was received with relief in some British quarters. It was seen by others as a bad omen.

❧

The *Standart* docked at Leith shortly before 10am. Queen Victoria had wanted to keep the arrival quiet and informal. Her flamboyant son Bertie, the Prince of Wales, had disagreed, writing to Bigge that he hoped his mother would: 'wish all honour to be done to them (the Emperor and Empress) in the eyes of the world, especially in those of Russia. I am so anxious that the arrival should be marked with every possible compliment for the Emperor.'

When Bertie had visited Russia, in 1866, for his sister-in-law's wedding to the future Tsar Alexander III, he had been treated to parades, banquets and a wolf hunt. His exuberance had won the Russians over, as he danced reels at the British embassy in full Highland dress, declaring himself: 'only too happy to be the means of promoting the entente cordiale between Russia and our own country'.

The Russians had much preferred Bertie to his more austere mother. The Queen, in her turn, never came round to the bear-like Tsar Alexander. She would not have been impressed by his ability to walk through doors without opening them or his virtuosity on the tuba. Indeed, she labelled him: 'a sovereign whom she does not look upon as a gentleman'. Nor would she have approved of his reactionary views: he deemed parliamentary government 'the great lie of our time'. She dismissed him finally as: 'barbaric, Asiatic and tyrannical'.

Following the death of Tsar Alexander, Bertie had returned to Russia, to support his sister-in-law, now the Dowager Empress. Some of the British party had found the elaborate funeral rituals overwhelming. Bertie's equerry complained to the Queen of: 'the 39th repetition of the same mass'. Bertie's son Georgie, later George V, wrote to his wife, May, of his unease: 'Every day, after lunch, we had another service at the church… after the service was over we all went up to the coffin, which was open and kissed the holy picture which he holds in his hand. It gave me a shock when I saw his dear face to close to mine.' Bertie, however, never grumbled, even after finding himself obliged to spend his 53rd birthday on a funeral cortège.

His efforts were acknowledged when he was awarded a Russian title: colonel in chief of the 27th Dragoon Regiment of Kiev. The Queen's Lord Chamberlain, Charles Carrington, was one of the first to see Bertie in his Russian uniform. He had not been impressed by the sight, feeling it called to mind: 'a fat man in a huge shaggy greatcoat looking like a giant polar bear'.

✦

Bertie won his argument regarding the Romanovs' welcome, and the ceremony featured six battleships, two cruisers and two gunboats. At a 21-gun salute, a flotilla of steamers, tugs and small boats rushed into the harbour. Cheering onlookers lined the decks of the larger vessels, while crowds of spectators gathered in the docks.

However, references to poor weather remained unavoidable. *The Times* paid a laconic tribute to the beleaguered crowd: 'An easterly wind was accompanied by drenching rain and for several hours there was a ceaseless downpour.' *The Scotsman* weighed in: 'It was one of those days that does Scotland no favours.' The Tsar wrote one of his cursory diary notes: 'The weather deteriorated… and it rained,' while Carington sent the Queen a series of stoic telegrams: 'Their majesties look remarkably well, unfortunately it is raining'… 'all well weather still rainy'… 'all went off admirably weather bad'.

It was Bertie, now 54, and his brother, Arthur, the Duke of Connaught, 46, who went to greet the young imperial couple on the *Standart*. The two men were brought out on a tender as the yacht was dropping anchor. The Queen had written to her son about the importance of greeting the Tsar: 'The arrivals at Leith being in State and your having met Nicky's grandfather (Alexander II) at Dover on the occasion of his visit in 1874 I think you could not do otherwise now.'

In the spirit of British and Russian harmony, Bertie and Nicky each wore the uniform of the other's country. There were mentions, in several accounts, of Bertie finding his Russian dragoons uniform uncomfortably small. He did have a weight problem, Queen Victoria herself wrote: 'He is grown so large and almost quite bald.' Her lady-in-waiting, Lady Edith Lytton, may have been protesting too much when she now insisted that his distinctive grey and red greatcoat was: 'not the least tight'.

Nicky had been appointed colonel in chief of the

Scots Greys at the time of his wedding, in 1894, writing an enthusiastic letter of thanks to 'Granny', as he called Queen Victoria: 'Words fail me to express my surprise and the pleasure I felt upon receiving the news that you had appointed me colonel in chief of the beautiful Royal Scots Greys, just the regiment I saw and admired so much last summer at Aldershot. I shall be happy and proud to appear one day before you in their uniform.'

In fact, it turned out that Nicky's discomfort almost matched his uncle's: he hated having to appear in front of his 350-man crew in the wrong outfit. As he complained in a letter to his mother: 'You will understand how unpleasant it was to have to say goodbye to our officers and crew in a foreign uniform.' The Tsar's favourite item of clothing was a long red shirt, less suited to Balmoral, or even the Russian court, than Old Muscovy.

To add to his difficulties, the Tsar did not agree with his fellow countrymen on the subject of Bertie. He found his 'dear U(ncle) Bertie' rather overbearing and may well have had mixed feelings as the pair exchanged greetings. During his visit to Britain for his cousin Georgie's wedding, three years before, he had described his reservations to his mother: 'Uncle Bertie is in very good spirits and very friendly, almost too much so.' Lady Lytton was struck by Bertie's ebullience, reporting that he was 'very nice to everyone all day'. Bertie was only too aware of the stark contrast between him and his quieter nephew, privately pronouncing Nicky: 'weak as water'.

Lunch was held on board the *Standart*. The Tsar sat at the head of the table, with the Tsarina on his left and the Duchess of Buccleuch on his right. Lady Lytton, then 54, and a former Vicereine of India, was painfully struck by the youth of the Tsar. 'One longed for haute politique to be discussed and when one looked at the very young Tsar it seemed more than ever ridiculous of the papers to say that all depended on him for decisions in the Eastern question.'

Nicky, then 28, was slight and, at 5ft 5, fractionally smaller than his wife; he had soft, delicate features. Alix's sharper features had a brittle, fragile quality. Lady Lytton added: 'There was no whispering and the Emperor and Empress being so young makes them so little alarming compared to old royalties.' At just before 2pm, the party boarded the tender to be taken ashore. Carington had earlier sent a telegram to Bigge: 'Vessel can't get alongside train at Leith so carriages necessary. Will the Queen lend her saloon carriages?'

The Tsar had turned down the original idea of a state procession along Edinburgh's Royal Mile. But he agreed to a welcoming ceremony at Leith and the Romanovs were duly greeted by the Lord Provost at Victoria Jetty, to the accompaniment of both national anthems. The jetty had been decorated with red, white and blue bunting, intertwined with imperial standards and black and gold ribbons. A telegram marked 'Very urgent' had been sent, on 16th September, from the secretary at the Russian embassy to the equerry-in-waiting at Balmoral: 'Russian national colours are red, blue, white, Russian imperial colours black and yellow'. The weather proved literally a dampener, as saturated decorations flapped limply in strong winds.

The guard of honour comprised members of the Argyll and Sutherland Highlanders and, of course, the Royal Scots Greys. Bertie had given Bigge a clear instruction: 'Prince of Wales submits the suggestion that the Scots Greys do greeting despite expense.'

The Lord Provost presented the imperial couple with an engraved golden box, while the wife of the provost of Leith gave the Tsarina a large bunch of orchids. Lady Lytton was not impressed by the imperial couple's responses: 'The Emperor very shyly whispered a few words of thanks but he ought to learn to do this sort of thing better. She smiles but neither of them takes trouble enough to bow to all assembled as our Queen did SO well.'

Lady Lytton couldn't have known that Alix, a martyr to real and imagined ailments, was in recovery from a debilitating headache. As the Tsar had recorded in his diary two nights before: 'I had dinner at 8pm with the officers – without Alix – she had a headache!' She had ended up spending the preceeding day in her cabin: 'Alix continued to stay in bed, afraid to get up.'

The couple were driven, in an open carriage, along North Junction Street to Leith railway station, cheered by the valiant crowd. As Carington had assured Bigge: '2,000 volunteers will line the whole route from Leith Port.' According to *The Times*, the young Tsarina wore a delicate white dress, large hat and a white ostrich feather boa. *The Graphic* compared the Tsarina's flimsy outfit unfavourably with the Duchess of Connaught's: 'Charming and graceful as the Russian Empress is, she alighted from one sea voyage in a… fawn mantle trimmed with white ostrich feather collar and a bonnet of white and blue… the Duchess of Connaught wore "a real English costume" – a dark brown tweed tailor-made dress and coat'.

The official paper giving instructions to the courtiers for

the journey, specified levee dress, as opposed to the more formal full dress. 'Levee dress will be worn at Leith and on arrival at Balmoral.' The men's coatees (tail coats), complete with embroidery on collar, cuffs and pocket flaps, would probably not have been much more waterproof than the Tsarina's fawn mantle.

Though barely visible, the heavily swaddled baby, Grand Duchess Olga, created her own sensation. *The Daily Telegraph* had made much of Olga's birth the previous November, insisting that the news was: 'received with much friendly interest in this country, where all that concerns the present and future of Russia is the subject of intelligent and sympathetic appreciation'.

The newspapers were, indeed, full of friendly interest, with *The Yorkshire Herald* declaring: 'The Grand Duchess takes very kindly to her new surroundings.' *The Huddersfield Chronicle* spoke of the Tsarina's 'pride and joy at having a little daughter to bring with her... almost pathetic to witness'. *The Leeds Mercury* was ecstatic: 'The sight of the imperial baby moved every female heart in the crowd and there was an animated display of pocket handkerchiefs.'

At Balmoral, the Queen continued with her monitoring of progress: 'Heard of Nicky and Alicky's safe disembarkation and of their departure from Leith'. At Leith station, the imperial couple boarded an 11-carriage train for the first leg of the journey to Ballater. The train would cross 'Scotland's Eiffel Tower', the new Forth Bridge, before travelling through Kirkcaldy, Cupar, Dundee, Arbroath, Montrose,

Lawrencekirk, Stonehaven and Aberdeen. Earlier Nicky had referred wistfully to his departure from the new yacht in his diary: 'We bid farewell to the marvellous *Standart*.' The Romanovs' subsequent rail journey proved every bit as arduous as he had feared. He gave particulars in his diary – 'cold, drizzling, shivering on the train' – adding more detail in a letter to his mother: 'The train was rather rocky, so that Alix was very nearly ill.'

When councillors heard that the train was to stop at Dundee station for water, they immediately organised a welcome committee. As the Dundee City Rifles played the Russian national anthem, Nicky stepped out on to the platform to receive a silver casket from the acting chief magistrate. The Tsar gave thanks, presumably in a shy whisper, before reboarding.

By late afternoon, the train had reached Ferryhill Junction, at Aberdeen, where the Russian party switched to the Great North of Scotland Railway. Officials here matched Dundee with a further reception, attended by a group of 100 dignitaries. Official instructions specified: 'Tea will be served at Ferryhill junction', but refreshments would have to be rushed, as the party arrived at 5.31, to depart at 5.50. The rumours of bomb threats had centred on this last leg of the journey, so special constables spent the 19 minutes searching compartments and checking passengers.

This second train arrived at Ballater at 7pm, by which time the station bunting was, as the Queen's physician, Sir James Reid, noted: 'sadly lashed' by rain. Bertie's son, Georgie, was waiting at the station, dressed, appropriately, in a kilt. The Tsar and Georgie were strikingly similar in appearance, with the same hairstyle, beard and moustache.

When the Queen first met Nicky, at Georgie's wedding, she had been struck by their general resemblance. 'Nicky', she wrote, 'is so charming and wonderfully like Georgie.' She cheerily noted that their physical likeness: 'led to no end of funny mistakes'.

Nicky had not been so thrilled: 'Everyone finds a great resemblance between Georgie and me. I am tired of hearing this again and again.' He was very fond of Georgie, but he may have been slightly relieved to hear that his doppel-gänger had been driven out of Balmoral by the crush of visitors. He and his wife, May, would be lodging down the road, at the estate of Glen Muick.

The beleaguered party now spent a further hour in the rain, travelling the last eight miles in five open carriages. The procession was led by the Scots Greys, followed by pipers, torchbearers and finally the carriages: one devoted solely to baby Olga and two attendants. Walking along-side were the Balmoral Highlanders and Crathie and Ballater Volunteers. Inspector Baxter of the Aberdeenshire Constabulary had given assurances that his rather meagre sounding contingent would be: 'in good time and properly dressed and in tidy order... Full dress uniform with white gloves and leggings will be worn... Covering the distance between Crathie Post Office and Balmoral: Inspector Leslie and six Constables'.

As the procession approached Balmoral, the sound of the church bells vied with the bagpipes playing 'The Campbells Are Coming'. A line of estate workers and kilted highlanders held burning torches along the roadside, while bonfires had been lit on the tops of the surrounding hills. The Marquis of Carisbrooke later pronounced the spectacle one of the 'most impressive sights' he'd ever witnessed. Fanciful postcards produced after the visit show the imperial party submerged in a smoky mist from the burning torches. A plume of smoke rises from a fire on the hill behind. As May called it, in a letter to her Aunt Augusta: 'a true highland welcome'.

With the growing darkness and continuing rain, the travellers must have been relieved, finally, to catch sight of Balmoral's distinctive crenulations and turrets. The Queen had always been very enthusiastic about the castle's appearance: 'New house looks beautiful', she wrote, when the royal family first moved in. 'An old shoe was thrown after us into the house for good luck when we entered the hall.' Her children had not always been so enamoured, her son Leopold proclaiming it: 'that most vile and abominable of places'. Upon arrival, the exhausted passengers disembarked, while kilted highlanders, according to one newspaper: 'silently filed off through the shrubbery'.

The Tsar had given the impression that he was very keen to see Balmoral. Earlier in the year, when the new Ambassador in Russia, Nicholas O'Connor, had discussed the possibility of a visit, he wrote: 'The Tsar recalled his happy days spent in Britain. The Empress has spoken to him so much about Balmoral he felt as if he were quite familiar with its beautiful surroundings.' The Tsar's clipped diary entry, that evening, however, made no mention of any beauty: 'arrived at Balmoral under torchlight toward 8pm'.

He and Victoria rival each other in the brevity of their accounts of the long-awaited reunion. The Queen wrote: 'We went down at 7.30pm into the visitors' room and waited there till we heard the church bells ringing and the pipers playing... I was standing at the door. Nicky got out

Fanciful postcards produced after the visit show the
imperial party submerged in a smoky mist

first and I embraced him, and then darling Alicky, all in
white, looking so well.' Nicky wrote: 'Granny with both the
ladies and the children's family staff personnel met us at the
door.' He did add, once again, slightly more detail in a letter
to his mother: 'Granny was waiting for us on the steps...
Marvellously kind and amiable to us... I don't think her
much changed except that she seemed a little smaller, just
as you found her.'

While the Tsar found that the Queen had got smaller,
she was delighted to report that Nicky and Alix were exactly
the same. The new Tsar and Tsarina, travel-weary and probably drenched, certainly did not appear to be giving themselves airs. As she enthused: 'Dear Nicky and Alicky are

quite unspoilt and unchanged, as dear and simple as ever and as kind as ever.'

※

There was no indication, at this point, that the Tsar was any more taken with Balmoral's interior than he had been by its exterior. The 70-room castle incorporated many of Prince Albert's designs and was strewn with his memorabilia. As the Queen had once described it: 'the place where everything, even down to the smallest detail is somehow associated with Him and His memory [sic]'. At the foot of the staircase was a full-size white marble statue of Albert. Antlers and hunting trophies contributed to what Georgie's wife, May, described as the castle's masculine atmosphere. Other such features included: 'a smell of wood fire, stags' heads (three shot by Albert) rugs, leather'.

As one author put it: 'Albert wed memories of German castles to his own taste and his love for Scotland.' There was tartan upholstery, curtains and carpets: the Prince had, at one point, even designed his own mauve and grey tartan. The profusion of thistles once inspired Lord Clarendon to declare: 'The thistles are in such abundance that they would rejoice the heart of a donkey if they happened to LOOK LIKE his favourite repast, which they don't.'

The imperial couple were shown into the drawing room for drinks. The drawing room itself was not universally popular. Lord Rosebery once brazenly said that he had believed the drawing room at Victoria's Osborne House, on the Isle of Wight, to be the ugliest in the world, till he saw its equivalent at Balmoral.

Perhaps it was fortunate that the visitors had little time to consider the decor before the momentous entrance of baby Olga. Queen Victoria was immediately entranced: 'The dear baby was then brought in, a most beautiful child and so big.' The Queen mentioned her granddaughter's generous proportions again to her daughter Vicky: 'The baby is magnificent... bigger than she or Ella [Alix and her sister Ella] ever were and a lovely lively [great] grandchild'. Her physician, Sir James Reid, was pleased to report that, at ten and a half months old, the imperial baby weighed 30^1/$_2$ pounds, minus the three and a half pounds of clothes she was wearing.

The Tsar noted proudly that Granny was 'delighted to see Olga'. The *Yorkshire Herald* pulled no punches: 'It is said that the moment she [Olga] saw her great grandmother she delighted that august lady by adopting her as her first and most willing slave.'

Though the Queen remained unexpansive, she did allow herself one of her brief, lyrical moments: 'After which [drinks] N and A went to their rooms and I quickly dressed for dinner, to which we went down just before nine... it seems quite like a dream having dear Alicky and Nicky here.' The couple's rooms had been painstakingly redecorated in imperial black and yellow. If the Tsar noticed the colours, he never mentioned them. His account of the evening centred on his relief at removing the controversial Scots Greys uniform: 'Dinner was at 9pm. I did not crawl out of my uniform before 11pm.'

Wednesday 23 September

Queen Victoria's diary: 'The morning was again hopelessly bad and the day continued wet till late in the afternoon.'

On that first day of the imperial couple's visit, Queen Victoria became the longest-reigning monarch. She claimed to be anxious to play it down: 'Today is the day on which I have reigned longer, by a day, than any reigning English sovereign and the people wished to make all sorts of demonstrations, which I asked them not to do, until I had completed the 60 years next June. But notwithstanding that this was made public in the papers people of all kinds and ranks from every part of the Kingdom sent congratulatory telegrams and they kept coming in all day.'

She was also, more controversially, marking the anniversary of the Fall of Sevastopol, in the Crimea, delighting in putting on a small exhibition of trophies won from the imperial Russian armies in 1855. According to A.N. Wilson, the imperial couple viewed the exhibits with 'humourless solemnity'.

The Tsar was not in good spirits. He was oppressed, first, by the continuing rain and, secondly, by work pressures that prevented him from unpacking properly. He was known for being fastidious, able to find pencils in his study, in the pitch dark. 'From morning on the weather remained atrocious,' he grumbled, 'the same as yesterday. I did not have time to unpack in my room, a messenger had brought my papers.' Furthermore, he missed out on sharing one of his favourite dishes, porridge oats, with the Queen. As she recorded: 'Only dear Alicky breakfasted with us and the sweet Baby was brought in.'

Little Olga had a rapturous reception. Lady Lytton was as smitten as the Queen, already insisting that Olga's social skills outshone her parents': 'Oh you never saw such a darling as she is... a very broad face, very fat, in a lovely high St Joshua baby bonnet – but with bright intelligent eyes, a wee mouth and so happy and contented the whole day... quite an old person already – bursting with life and happiness and a perfect knowledge how to behave.'

The Tsar was usually an enthusiastic huntsman. The Ambassador, Nicholas O'Connor, had written to Bigge on 9th September: 'I gather that the Emperor is looking forward to a really quiet time at Balmoral, to killing some grouse and stags, he is looking forward to some rest and repose after all he has been through.' In fact, when he reached Balmoral, he was curiously reluctant, complaining to his mother: 'From the very first day, my uncles took charge of me... they seem to think it necessary to take me out shooting all day with the gentlemen. The weather is awful, rain and wind every day.'

It is hard to know what exactly put the Tsar off. Was it really the unpleasant conditions? Was it his resentment of time spent away from his beloved wife? Or was it simply that he dreaded the prospect of long hours with his over-bearing uncles? Whatever the case, he was clearly relieved by the failure of that first outing: 'In addition the uncles wanted to drag me off to hunt grouse. But this all fell apart due to the weather.'

Lunch was served at 1pm, as the Queen recorded baldly: 'We lunched in the dining room.' Neither the Tsar nor the Tsarina were bon viveurs. They would have been unfazed by Balmoral's more spartan traditions, not least meals gobbled down in half an hour, occasionally in silence.

The food, equally, would have held little interest. Over time, the Tsarina may well have developed an appetite for the local produce so savoured by the Queen: salmon and trout from the river Dee and venison from the estate. Left to her own devices, however, she was happy to eat chicken cutlets twice daily for months on end. Her husband had his own simple preferences: beetroot or cabbage soup.

Granny's strictures on smoking, however, would have been more controversial. The chain-smoking Tsar would have been horrified to find himself reduced to smoking in a specially designated room, accessible only through an open kitchen courtyard. This smokers' room was sparsely furnished and kept intentionally cold; malingerers were cleared out at 12.00 midnight sharp, with the extinguishing of the lights. Two years before, while staying with the Queen at Windsor, the Tsar had complained of an evening during which: 'We talked until 11pm which, due to standing and not having the possibility to smoke, drove me to complete exhaustion.'

By the end of lunch, the weather had cleared and plans for outings were resumed. As the Queen recorded blithely: 'Nicky, the others and some of the gentlemen went out for a deer drive in the Abergeldie woods.' This delayed shoot bore out the Tsar's worst expectations: 'Six for lunch at 1pm and then we went off to the nearby mountains to hunt deer. I did not see a thing.' His report of Uncle Bertie's better luck had a slightly sour ring; Bertie, he wrote, bagged 'an unlucky deer'.

He made no reference to his first sight of Balmoral's picturesque groves of fir and beech or the glades of hare-bells, daisies and heather. Nor was there any word of the statues and seats dedicated to faithful retainers and dogs.

The Queen and her granddaughter undertook a less challenging carriage outing. As the Queen put it: 'Took a short drive with Alicky and it was quite fair.' Whether it really was 'quite fair' is impossible to know. Drives usually went ahead in fog, rain and snow, with the Queen readily switching her satin slippers for sturdy boots. She had always been averse to changing routines. As her acerbic lady-in-waiting, Marie Mallet, wrote: 'There seems a curious charm to our beloved Sovereign in doing the same thing on the same day year after year.' According to one description of Balmoral, the same chairs were kept in the same places and the same biscuits on the same plates. The only items to be replaced were the dogs, when they died.

The Queen continued merrily: 'Had tea on coming home and it seemed quite like old times seeing her [Alix] sitting there.' Her granddaughter may well have been trying to forget old times. Seven years previously, Alix had had an awkward stay at Balmoral with Bertie's eldest son, Prince Albert. The Prince, known, confusingly, as Eddie, had been earmarked by the Queen as a match for Alix. If that match failed, she declared, she would try Eddie's brother, Georgie. As she wrote to her daughter, Vicky: 'My heart and mind are bent on securing dear Alicky for either Eddie or Georgie.'

The Queen had always taken a passionate interest in her granddaughter's marital prospects, considering herself in loco parentis following the death of Alix's mother, Alice. The Princess had been just six when her mother died. The Queen's first priority had been to stop Alix marrying a Russian. As she instructed Vicky: 'You must prevent FURTHER Russians or other people coming to snap her up.' She informed Alix crisply that her late mother would not have countenanced a Russian match: 'Dear Mama said she would never hear of it.'

The Queen had invited Alix and Eddie to stay at Balmoral together, and a courtship of sorts had followed. Indeed Eddie had appeared to be devastated when Alix turned him down. It is hard, however, to gauge the extent of his hurt, as the young Prince was known for being both feckless and homosexual. James Pope-Hennessy dismissed him as 'heedless and aimless as a gleaming goldfish in a crystal ball'. He died suddenly, three years later, of complications following a bout of flu.

The truth was that Alix was already bound up with Nicky. Their mutual fascination had sparked when Alix was just 12, becoming serious when she was 17. The couple had faced opposition from both sides, with Nicky's father, Alexander III, denouncing Alix as: 'too German altogether'. Members of the English community in St Petersburg seemed to share his distaste. One of the Princess of Wales' ladies-in-waiting, Charlotte Knollys, wrote a scathing letter from St Petersburg, in which she dismissed Alix as 'a little scrubby Hessian Princess.'

Tsar Alexander's objections were, however, no more effective than the Queen's. The couple's engagement took

The Tsarina at Balmoral

place on 20th April 1894, or 8th April, according to the Russian calendar. Nicky's diary entry was fond but matter-of-fact: 'A marvellous unforgettable day in my life – the day of my engagement with dear, beloved Alix.' His new fiancée's entry was characteristically gushing: 'Ap [sic] 20th Easternight! Shall we ever forget it, oh, my kind sweet mannykins – toi, toi, toi, toi.'

The thwarted Queen admitted that she was 'thunderstruck': 'I knew that Nicky much wished it, I thought that Alicky was not sure of her mind.' She made no secret of the efforts she had made to prevent the marriage, lamenting to her daughter, Vicky: 'I had laboured so hard to PREVENT it and I felt there was NO LONGER any danger and all in one night EVERYTHING was changed.'

Fortunately, with all her objections to Russians generally,

the Queen always retained a soft spot for Nicky. As she put it to Vicky: 'The more I think of sweet Alicky's marriage the more unhappy I am. NOT as to the personality, for I like him very much.'

The pair had enjoyed their first substantial meeting at Windsor at the time of Georgie's wedding in 1893. The Queen had stationed herself at the top of a staircase, before processing slowly down the steps. Sensitive about his height, to the point of walking on tiptoe, Nicky may well have disliked having to crane his neck. But he maintained his sangfroid, boldly comparing her, later, to: 'a round ball with wobbly legs'. She, in turn, pronounced him: 'very simple and unaffected'.

She was immediately impressed by his language skills: 'Nicky… always speaks English and almost without a fault.' When he returned to England after his engagement to Alix she set about cultivating his tutor, Charles Heath, inviting him to Osborne and pumping him for reports: 'After luncheon I again saw good old Mr Heath and had some interesting conversation with him. He spoke in the highest terms of Nicky, who he said was excellent and true.' Mr Heath's good opinion of Nicky was not reciprocated. The young Tsarevich had been highly amused by the Romanov family parrot's impersonation of him. As his sister, Olga, recorded: 'Every time the poor master entered… the bird would fly into a rage and then imitate Mr Heath with the most exaggerated British accent. Mr Heath finally became so exasperated that he refused to enter Georgie's room until Popka had been removed.'

Nicky's decision to talk to the Queen soon after the announcement of his engagement proved particularly popular. 'Afterwards Nicky came and had some talk with me in my room. He is so sensible and nice, and expressed the hope to come quietly to see Alicky at the end of June.' He gleefully described how she had summoned her Indian servant, 'the Munshi', to share the news. 'She [the Queen] called for the Munshi, her teacher of the Indian language, and he congratulated me on the occasion of my engagement.'

There were 22 for dinner including Colonel Arthur Davidson, groom-in-waiting in ordinary to the Queen, and Carington, still smarting from his brushes with the Russian naval attaché. The Queen embarked on what Nicky might have regarded as ominous talks with the Russian Ambassador, Baron George de Staal: As she reported: 'After dinner spoke to M de Staal about public affairs... said it would be a very good thing if I spoke to Nicky on all the important points'.

Thursday 24th September

The Tsar's diary: 'At last the weather improved and all the mountains were wiped clean of the storm clouds which had hung over them... I had a walk with Alix.'

The Tsar was delighted by the weather, relieved to have a reprieve from his uncles and thrilled to spend time with his wife. As the imperial couple walked, they savoured their freedom from the rigorous security arrangements foisted on them in St Petersburg. They may well have thought back to the early months of their engagement, mostly spent in Britain.

The pair had been separated for six weeks when Nicky was obliged to return to Russia. During his absence, Alix had succumbed to a bout of sciatica and been advised to go for a cure in Harrogate. Her intention had been to remain incognito, staying in an obscure boarding house, under the name of Baroness Starckenburg. However, her real identity soon became known. Her insistence that her landlady's newborn twins be named Nicholas and Alix may not have helped. She elected herself the twins' godmother, subsequently sending Nicholas Allen a confirmation present of cufflinks by Fabergé.

Periods between cures were taken up with her tutor, Catherine Schneider, and a crate of Russian manuals. She gamely described her sessions with Miss Schneider as 'amusing but certainly not easy'. She found the presence of her second companion, her nine-year-old niece, Alice, a welcome relief. She also enjoyed a visit from Alice's mother, her much-loved sister, Victoria. Worries about sciatica were cast aside as Alix, her sister and niece raced around town on tricycle bath chairs.

After weeks of cures and Russian lessons, Alix would have been looking forward to a reunion with her fiancé. The couple were finally reunited in what the Tsar referred to as Victoria's 'little house', the actually very substantial Elm Grove, in Walton-on-Thames. Victoria had by then been married to Prince Louis of Battenberg for ten years and the couple had three children. Their fourth child, Louis, the future Lord Mountbatten, was not yet born.

Nicky's diary account was predictably sparse and included a familiar allusion to dispiriting weather: 'I arrived at "Walton" in 25 minutes and at 3.45 met dear Alix. Again I experienced the happiness which I had when I left Coburg! It is a rare, warm and friendly life for four people in Victoria's and Ludwig's little house. We spent the rest of the day together at home, since it was pouring.'

The betrothed couple shared some of their first blissful moments together at 'Walton'. During bursts of sunshine, they lazed under a chestnut tree, near the river bank, or took boating trips. Nicky, a poor sailor, relished the gentle demands of the Thames, enthusing about their first excursion 'up to the town of Camden' on an 'electric dinghy': 'The outing turned out superb, the riverbanks are beautiful... I was in ecstasy over everything that had been built along the riverbanks.' Their second jaunt was on a rowing boat or, as Nicky called it: 'a comfortable gig'. As they stopped for tea on a riverbank, Nicky proudly noted his future wife's unexpected catering skills: '[We] started to boil up some tea. Alix did all of this, since she has an excellent new "tea basket" from Granny.'

There were tensions, though. The couple found themselves contending with the high spirits of young Alice and her sister Louise (the future Queen of Sweden), about which Nicky registered his irritation: 'The girls romped around terribly in the carriage.' He and Alice never altogether hit it off. She would later quote his tremulous words during a drive through Windsor Park. According to Alice, he said: 'I really dread becoming Tsar because I shall never hear the truth again.' Even as a child she viewed his thoughts as 'defeatist'. Her memory of her Aunt Alix contrasts starkly with subsequent descriptions of the Tsarina: 'We all loved her, she was so delighted and happy.'

⚜

The Tsar summed up the couple's precious stroll at Balmoral in a brief sentence: 'We stopped by the only shop here and bought a few incidentals.' The owners of the only shop, grandly entitled 'The Merchants', were two elderly sisters, and the 'incidentals' might have been anything from tartans or notebooks to pastries. The sisters had once taught Alix how to make traditional Scottish scones and she had taken the recipe with her to St Petersburg. Her skill with scones could have been usefully combined with her mastery of Granny's 'tea basket'.

Upon their return, Nicky and Alix enjoyed what the Queen referred to as 'a large luncheon', attended by cousin Georgie and his wife, May. Georgie, at this point, echoed his grandmother's view of the new Tsar as unchanged: 'Had a good talk with dear Nicky. He is just the same dear boy as he always was.' Despite the age difference – Georgie was three years older than Nicky – the cousins had always been close. Their friendship had been forged in Denmark, during happy holidays orchestrated by their Danish mothers.

Georgie had written an especially affectionate letter after hearing of Nicky's engagement. He had been among those who voiced misgivings about the match, but his centred solely on the cousins' shared lack of height. He had raised the ticklish subject with Alix, who then complained to her fiancé: 'Foolish Georgie says I am to insist upon you wearing high heels and that I am to have quite low ones. May won't change hers, but he wears much higher ones. At first they had been uncomfortable, now he did not mind it any more.'

Bertie's wife, the future Queen Alexandra, arrived at Balmoral that second afternoon, with her daughter, Princess Victoria. The pair had suffered an arduous journey, as the Tsar reported with concern: 'At 4pm Aunt Alix arrived with Victoria; they had had an absolutely terrible crossing on the *Osborne*.' The Queen made her own sympathetic reference to their: 'frightful passage from Copenhagen'.

After commiserating with Aunt Alexandra and Victoria, the party visited the Castle of Braemar, before stopping at one of the Queen's so-called hideaway cottages, the 'Dantzig', for tea.

While insisting that the Romanovs' Balmoral visit was of a purely personal and domestic nature, *The Times* admitted that: 'Coming at a critical juncture in European politics, the visit of the Tsar has been invested with singular importance.' Certainly, Granny, perhaps prompted by her talk with the Ambassador the previous evening, made the most of her time with the young Tsar. It was during the return carriage ride from the 'Dantzig' that she broached her most pressing topic: 'I said a few words to him about Turkey and Armenia, saying his own Ambassador at Constantinople... hoped some agreement would be come to whilst Nicky was here, as affairs were very critical and some catastrophe was dreaded... I remarked that if England and Russia went together there must be peace and something must be done to bring this about.' The Tsar, she reported, remained characteristically agreeable and non-committal: 'Nicky said he quite saw this and would see what he could do'. She later added: 'Nicky nodded but said it would be difficult.'

Intent on avoiding what he gloomily labelled 'political conversations', the Tsar made no reference in his diary to Granny's unwelcome overtures or his response: 'At 5.30 we went off to have tea in one of the forest cottages. Dinner at 9pm.'

Friday 25th September

The Queen's diary: 'A dull morning, raining again... it was very cold.' For all her insistence that she was not celebrating her long reign, she was happy to boast: 'The congratulatory telegrams are still coming in.'

Having missed the preceding day, the hunters were keen to resume shooting. As the Queen wrote breezily: 'Nicky and the others came in to wish us good morning before going to a deer drive.'

If the Tsar was finding the company of his uncles generally oppressive, he particularly dreaded Bertie's repeated attempts to discuss an Anglo-Russian or Saxe-Coburg-Gotha-Romanov alliance. He preferred the company of his less enterprising cousin: 'I'm glad Georgie comes out to shoot too – we can at least talk over the good times we've just had in Denmark.'

The Tsar's second hunt went no better than the first. This despite his thoughtful hosts ensuring that he was in the best spot. As he wrote in his diary: 'Again it rained for half the day, but nevertheless we went off hunting to the place where we had tea yesterday… and on top of it no luck at all – I haven't killed a stag yet.' He managed somehow to blame the deer: 'For me the hunt was unsuccessful. I did shoot, but the deer were passing through far off.'

A record still exists of that particular deer drive:

> Emperor of Russia – 0
> Duke of Connaught – 4 stags
> Duke of York – 5 stags
> Prince of Wales – 0 (no shot)

The Tsarina later lamented to her former governess, Madgie: 'My husband has not shot one stag, only a brace of grouse.' The grouse would not, in fact, be bagged for a further three days.

The Tsar's spirits seemed to lift a little with lunch al fresco: 'Open air lunch, the weather had become better.' Back at the house, the Queen and Alix's more civilised lunch was followed by an informal concert: 'After luncheon', the Queen reported, 'Tostie, his wife and Wolff came up to my room and played and sang for Alicky, who was there.' Paolo Tosti was an Italian composer who had acted as a singing master for the royal family. Alix would have been relieved to be listening rather than performing. Though a keen pianist, she hated playing in public, insisting that it had been one of the worst ordeals of her life. As a child, she had been forced to perform by the Queen; she complained that her 'clammy hands felt literally stuck to the keys'.

There were those in the royal household who deemed the imperial couple aloof, though Alix, understandably more at ease in her grandmother's house, made several conquests. One of the Queen's ladies-in-waiting singled her out as: 'unmistakably lovely... one is always in rapture with her'.

Lady Lytton was won over as Alix confided her worries about nannies: 'The Empress talked to me a long time after dinner and was so nice. Like anyone else she has had nurse troubles and the first she had was rude and domineering, never even bowing to the Emperor. The one she has now is a housekeeper in a Russian family and she cannot keep her, but she is nice.'

Alix's first 'English nurse' had, in fact, been specially selected for her by the Queen. Mrs Inman had first appeared at the palace the previous December, when little Olga was nearly five weeks old. Nicky took an instant dislike to her, which may well have had something to do with her refusal to bow to him. In any case, he complained to his brother Georgie: 'She has something hard and unpleasant in her face and looks like a stubborn woman.' He and Alix were agreed, he added, they: 'did not like the look of Mrs Inman'.

The Tsar subsequently included some neutral references to her in his diary, writing on 20th December: 'After tea we attended the little daughter's bath – the nanny, Mrs Inman, gave her a bath.' But he was soon back on the attack, telling his brother that Alix was worried 'the new English nanny would in some way affect the way of things in our daily family life'. The daily family life was, indeed, affected when Mrs Inman made the unpopular decision to move baby Olga into the nursery upstairs.

The Tsarina mentioned her growing dislike of Mrs Inman to her own brother, Ernie. She found Mrs Inman's fondness for impersonations particularly distasteful: 'I am NOT AT ALL enchanted with the nurse…. she is good and kind with Baby, but as a woman most antipathetic and that disturbs me sorely. Her manners are neither very nice and she will mimic people in speaking about them, an odious habit wh[ich] would be awful for a child to learn – most headstrong (but I am too, thank goodness) I foresee no end of troubles and only wish I had another.'

The Queen's endorsement protected Mrs Inman for four months, but the imperial couple's brothers would both, doubtless, have been relieved to hear that, on 29th April, she had been given her marching orders. The Tsar wrote with uncharacteristic candour: 'Today the unbearable nanny left us – the English woman; we are glad that we are finally separated from her!'

Her successor, the 'nice' housekeeper from a Russian family, was one of two English sisters, the Misses Coster, who both worked for members of the Romanov dynasty. The first worked for the Tsar's sister, Xenia, eventually tending all seven children. The second arrived at the palace three days after the departure of Mrs Inman. The Tsar did not find this Miss Coster hard-faced, but he was struck by another peculiarity in her appearance. On 2nd May 1896 he wrote: 'After tea I walked upstairs to watch little daughter's bath. Since yesterday a new nanny has been tending to her – a nurse from Kseniya Institute, with a very long nose, who has been taken on, until she proves otherwise.' 'Mrs Coster' was written into the diary margin by Alix.

Unmarried nannies would often be known, decorously, as Mrs.

The Tsar's sister, Olga, recalled another disastrous nanny: 'My niece Olga's nurse was a terror – fond of tippling. In the end she was found in bed with a Cossack and dismissed on the spot.'

Perhaps any nanny at the Russian court would have a hard time matching Alix's own English nurse, Orchie. Mary Ann Orchard, in fact a Dubliner – and another of Queen Victoria's protégées – had tended Alix from the time of her birth, looking after her as she faced the deaths of her mother and two siblings. Over the years, Orchie would vie for Alix's affection with Madgie (Margaret Jackson), the more sophisticated, London-born governess who would later be credited with teaching Alix to think independently. Sadly, for all Madgie's acclaimed fondness for abstract thought, the Tsarina would become known for her failure to grasp the wider picture, and her refusal to have it explained to her by anybody else.

Orchie, by then aged 64, followed Alix to Russia in 1894, helping her to dress on her wedding day. Another of the Tsarina's sisters, Irene, wrote to the Queen describing a visit to the palace shortly after Orchie's arrival: 'Orchie was bustling about with the rest of all her things… it looked so homelike.' After Olga's birth, Orchie took overall charge of the nursery. Alix's sister Victoria assured the Queen that Orchie was an immediate hit with Olga: 'The baby is magnificent – a bright intelligent little soul – she is especially fond of Orchie, smiling broadly whenever she catches sight of her.'

The prolonged conversation about nannies at Balmoral

would have confirmed the ascerbic lady-in-waiting Marie Mallet's worst misgivings about the Tsarina. She later described Alix as: 'The angelic but somewhat cowlike Princess who he [the Tsar] adores but who cares for little beyond her husband and her children'. Mallet went on to dismiss Alix, more savagely, as: 'a rabid, pathetic hausfrau' who 'cannot rouse herself to reform either society or politics'. Her pronouncements on Nicky carried echoes of Uncle Bertie's: she denounced him as a 'weakling'.

The Tsar's fourth night seems to have been mercifully uneventful: 'We had tea at the end of the hunt in Donald Stewart's house – an old hunter, who goes around with me during round-ups. Granny, Alix and others arrived there. Dinner at 9pm. In the evening I had writing to do.'

Saturday 26th September
Queen Victoria's diary: 'A fair day… much milder than yesterday.'

The Tsar commented on the welcome break in the downpours. Sadly, it did nothing to improve a second all-day hunt: 'It was a day without rain. At 11am the tireless hunters went off to the mountains for a beating-out, but no one saw any deer and for the whole day only one shot was heard. Lunch in the woods.'

While the Tsar dined under the trees, the Queen and Alix enjoyed a thoroughly domestic lunch, with an assortment of great-grandchildren. As the Queen wrote: 'Only ourselves and the little children to luncheon. Georgie's dear little boys came in, as well as little Olga.'

It is hard to know how close Alix became to Georgie's wife, May, but as young mothers of babies the same age, they shared a vital connection. May's eldest child, David, the future Edward VIII, was just over two years old. Nicky and Alix had visited him, when he was newly-born, in June 1894, and were made godparents. May's second son, Bertie, the future George VI, and the baby, Olga, had barely a month between them. The young mothers were additionally both pregnant again. May was expecting her third child, Victoria, while Alix was already pregnant with her second daughter, Tatiana, who was born the following June.

The toddler, David, and little Olga certainly bonded: a 'belle alliance' was declared as David purportedly picked Olga up, after a fall, and gave her a kiss.

The Prime Minister, Lord Salisbury, arrived that morning. He was keen to establish his own belle alliance with the Tsar, hopeful that the recent death of the tricky Foreign Minister, Lobanov-Rostovsky, might mitigate in his favour. The Tsar, anxious to maintain a holiday spirit, may well have heard news of the arrival with a sinking heart.

The Queen had always been more than happy to receive prime ministers with their dispatch boxes at Balmoral. The system did, however, have its detractors. Disraeli complained bitterly about the Queen: 'carrying on the government of the country 600 miles from the metropolis'.

Salisbury's complaints were less about the distance than

the accommodation. No amount of talks with the Tsar could quite compensate the 66-year-old Prime Minister for a freezing bedroom. His aide sent a note insisting the room be heated at 60 degrees, the highest temperature the Queen would allow. The request was marked 'private' and slipped in at the end of a letter: 'I am sure you will forgive my mentioning it, but it is most necessary that Lord Salisbury's room should be very warm: a minimum temperature of 60 degrees... I am ashamed to bother you with so trifling a matter but it is not as trifling as it may seem.'

Balmoral was notorious among members of the court for its lack of creature comforts. As one household member wrote: 'I never remember one congenial day in the Highlands.' Lord Clarendon, who had objected to the thistle motifs, claimed he suffered from frostbite during dinner. He described two sticks in the fireplace hissing at the servant trying to light them. The glacial temperatures sometimes proved too much even for the bullish Marie Mallet: 'The wind was so cold my face turned first blue then crimson and by dinner time I looked as if I had been drinking hard for a week – and this was in June.' Lady Lytton was less bothered by the temperature than the lack of space in her bedroom: 'One could hardly move when the two boxes were brought in.'

After an interlude with her great-grandchildren, the Queen was more than ready for a return to business. She set about engineering talks between the Prime Minister and the Tsar. If she was aware of Nicky's distaste for 'political conversations', she was not going to let this stand in her way. As she reported: 'Afterwards I saw Lord Salisbury, who had arrived early this morning. I told him how well disposed Nicky was and how anxious to speak to him.'

She gave an account, in her diary, of the Prime Minister's views on Turkey, the topic on which she had already lectured Nicky: 'What Lord Salisbury is anxious to avoid is anything which could appear as an attack on the Mahomedans, or encouragement of a propaganda against Muslims, which would be most dangerous on account of the enormous number of our Mahomedan subjects. He fears that the only thing which could do any good would be the removal of the Sultan.'

Sunday 27th September
Queen Victoria's diary: 'Pouring wet morning... fine but cold and inclined to be frosty'.
The Tsar grimly recorded an end to the dry spell: 'We woke up to awful weather – a rainstorm. At 12 o'clock we went to church; for the first time I attended a Scottish service.'

Just 15 months before, the Queen had been present at the opening and dedication of the new Craithie Kirk. The cost of the building had been met by donations and the proceeds of a curious two-day bazaar at Balmoral. The Queen had attended the bazaar twice, doubtless gratified to see several princesses tending stalls. The eight-year-old Ena of

Battenberg was particularly captivating as an 'old woman' selling dolls from a giant shoe. Photographic studies were taken for five shillings a time and goods on sale ranged from a plough for £50 to a penny 'leather scrubber'. The takings were a majestic £2,400.

For all the grand sums raised, Craithie Kirk remained a modestly sized, plain church, and Lady Lytton was struck by the sight of the royal parties in such humble surroundings: 'Very interesting seeing the two pews full of the royalties and the Emperor and Empress standing by the Queen even in the Scotch [church] where all is simple and reverend'. Their attendance impressed even Marie Mallet: 'She [the Queen] admired the Greek church most outside her own as being far more tolerant. For instance the Tsar and Tsarina went to Scotch service here, a thing no Roman Catholic monarch would ever do.'

Beyond saying that the Scotch service was his first, the Tsar made no comment. If he was underwhelmed by the sermon, he would have been in good company. As Lady Lytton reported: 'The prayer for their majesties was good, but the sermon so dull I could not say what it was.' They would both, however, have been in disagreement with the Queen, who expressed herself thoroughly satisfied: 'The service was performed by Dr. Colin Campbell of Dundee, who preached very well.'

Religion had always been a vital part of Alix's life. Her reluctance to give up her childhood Lutheranism and convert to orthodoxy had remained, for some time, an obstacle to her marrying Nicky. The Queen had raised the subject with the young Tsarevich soon after the couple's engagement: 'Nicky said: "She is much too good for me." I told him he must make the religious difficulties as easy as he could for her, which he promised to do.'

The Queen had been unexpectedly taken with the Russian priest charged with Alix's instruction. Her disapproval of Nicky's father, Alexander III, did not, apparently, extend to his choice of chaplain. As she wrote in her diary after the couple became engaged: 'Frogmore as usual for breakfast… went to the cottage where I saw the Russian priest Yanicheff, whom Nicky presented and who is reading with Alicky and preparing her for her entry into the Russian church. He is a very fine looking man with long grey hair and beard… He is the chaplain to the Emperor [Alexander III] and the imperial family and seems to be a very enlightened and wide-minded man.'

A few months after the wide-minded Yanicheff met Queen Victoria, he was at Tsar Alexander's death-bed.

❦

The gentle Sunday schedule at Balmoral continued with lunch, followed by tea at a neighbouring castle. As the Tsar wrote: 'Lunch with the family. It cleared up and became cold. I went for a walk to Abergeldie Castle, where we all had tea.' Religious services and walks were the stuff of Nicky's life. Upon his return, however, he would have been less happy to find himself buttonholed by the Prime Minister for a 'political conversation' lasting a full hour and a half: 'I had a talk with Salisbury,' he reported bleakly.

The talk centred, once again, on Turkey. Salisbury suggested that Russia and Britain should act together as a stabilising force. His appeal to the autocratic Tsar on moral and humanitarian grounds was later deemed ironic by leftist factions. Nicky, oblivious to such nuances, seemed pleased with the proposal. He was not averse, he declared, to putting pressure on the Sultan.

Subsequent talks about the Straits did not go quite so well. Nicky didn't like the idea of the Straits being open to all shipping; he was worried about foreign warships getting into the Black Sea. Using a well-worn cliché, he told Salisbury the Straits were: 'the door to the room in which he lived and he wanted the key'.

⁂

His later boast, in a letter to his mother, of 'very serious talks' had some justification. The letter's concluding comment, however, was wide of the mark: 'It's good at least for him [the Prime Minister] to learn from the source what the opinions and views of Russia are.'

Still reeling from his grapple with international politics, the Tsar now found himself facing more immediate concerns. The British authorities had decided that it would be too risky to allow the Romanovs to travel through London on their return journey; the Tsar was obliged to notify the Queen's former equerry, General Lynedoch Gardiner, that a London meeting was out of the question.

An aide, D. Galitzine, wrote a letter, dated 27th September, on the Tsar's behalf: 'I am requested by HIM the Emperor to communicate to you that His Majesty regrets very much that he will not have the pleasure of seeing you during his present stay in England as he will not go to London and in leaving Balmoral he will go straight to

Portsmouth to board the imperial yacht.'

Was he unsettled by having to dictate such a letter? Did he worry about its implications? He wound up his diary entry blandly enough: 'Dinner at 9pm and in the evening I worked'.

Monday 28th September
Queen Victoria's diary: 'A fine morning'.

The following day began well for the Tsar. He appeared curiously happy to set off early with the hunters. Was it just the improvement in the weather? Or could he have decided that, on balance, his uncles' company was preferable to Salisbury's? Whichever was the case, he was jubilant as, on this fourth shoot, he managed to bag two grouse: 'At last this was the first clear day. At 9.30 we went off to beat out some famous grouse on the hills around Birkhall and Glenmuich. In all, I killed two of them, since shooting these birds is very difficult.'

Describing his subsequent meal with 'numerous people', however, he reverted to reticent form: 'We had lunch in a tent courtesy of Lord Glenesk, at whose home we had tea at the end of our hunt.' And for all his triumph with the grouse, he still managed a grumble: 'I was tired enough from climbing around the hills and from standing on my feet for a long time in rooms inside earthen towers.'

Meanwhile, the Queen took her granddaughter back to The Merchants' shop. As she reported in her diary:

General
Lynedoch Gardiner
Thatched House Lodge
Richmond Park
Kingston on Thames.

27th September
1896.

Dear General Gardiner,

I am requested by H. I. M. the Emperor to communicate to you that His Majesty regrets very much that He will not have the pleasure of seeing you during His present stay in England as He will not go to London, and in leaving Balmoral He will go straight to Portsmouth on board the Imperial Yacht.

With sincere regrets of not having the pleasure of meeting you this time I beg to believe me, dear General. Your's most truly

D. Gatytzin

The Tsar's letter to General Gardiner

'Went to the village where they all went into a shop'. Alix apparently now filled her basket with the sisters' tartans, pastries and candies.

After lunch, the two ladies were joined, once again, by the great-grandchildren. The Queen's new-found passion for little Olga ran second only to her devotion to her great-grandson, David. The toddler was allowed all sort of liberties. As she enthused: 'Dear little David, with the baby, came in at the end of luncheon to say goodbye. David is a most attractive little boy and so forward and clever. He always tries at luncheon time to pull me up out of my chair, saying "Get up Gangan" and then to one of the Indian servants, "Man, pull it," which makes us laugh very much.'

Soon after tea, the Queen spoke to Salisbury, who told her that he had made progress in his talks with Nicky. She reported triumphantly that Salisbury had been: 'much struck by his [Nicky's] great candour and desire to be on the best terms with us'. Salisbury was later overheard praising the Tsar in general, telling Georgie that he was: 'very different from the other Emperor [the German Kaiser]!'

Included at dinner was the writer Donald Mackenzie Wallace, who would later become extra-groom-in-waiting to Bertie. Wallace had lived in Russia and in 1877 published two volumes of books entitled *Russia*. He had acted as political officer for Nicky during his tour of India in 1891. A more controversial guest was, once again, the Russian Ambassador, George de Staal. Rumour had it that the Ambassador collared Nicky at some point that evening, persuading him to rethink the assurances he had given Salisbury the day before.

Tuesday 29th September
Queen Victoria's diary: 'Rather dull'.
The Tsar wrote a cheerful report in his diary. 'The day was free, that is, without going out of the house to hunt.'

In fact, the Tsar's seventh day at Balmoral turned out to be anything but free. The morning was taken up with posing for the Queen's photographers, W. and D. Downey. The Tsar was obliged, once again, to put on his British uniform: 'I had my picture taken in the uniform and coat of the Scots Greys.' He was photographed with Arthur, the Duke of Connaught, both wearing identical uniforms. The Tsar looks nervous, his right hand grasping his left. The Duke of Connaught also seems ill at ease, as though his tunic is too well fitted about the waist. They both look earnestly at the camera.

The two men were subsequently joined by the rest of the royal party, including Bertie. As the Tsar wrote: 'The family came from Mar Lodge for lunch; they had their picture taken as a group.' The Queen added: 'Was photographed with Nicky, Alicky, Little Olga and Bertie'. The resulting photographs also seem curiously joyless. The Tsarina appears nervous and put-upon, while clutching Olga, who is making a face. The Tsar, still in the unpopular Scots Greys uniform, looks grimly at the camera. The Queen is

Tsar Nicholas with the Duke of Connaught

the only one looking at the baby; but she looks like she's delivering an admonishment. Bertie looks into the middle distance, as though wishing he were elsewhere.

The afternoon was busy and stressful. The Tsar found himself ensnared in a second talk with the Prime Minister: 'I had an additional conversation with Salisbury,' he wrote in dismay.

As far as Salisbury was concerned, this 'additional conversation' was distinctly unsatisfactory. The Tsar had

Queen Victoria with 'Nicky, Alicky, little Olga and Bertie'

the reputation of being very impressionable, echoing the opinions of the last person he had spoken to, frequently his adored wife. Salisbury was now convinced that the Tsar was voicing De Staal's views from the night before. He found Nicky altogether less agreeable, particularly on the subject of Turkey. He reported that the Tsar had changed his mind and was: 'distinctly averse, at this stage, to any effort to dethrone the Sultan'.

Salisbury added that, as the pair discussed a further topic, Egypt, Nicky seemed about to say he had no objection to a British occupation: 'But he stopped suddenly and turned the conversation as though he felt he was committing an imprudence.'

The Prime Minister later discussed the Tsar's propensity for 'conversation turning' with the Queen. She remained optimistic, convinced that Nicky would always, finally, be on side. As she reported: 'Regarding the Sultan, he [Salisbury] saw that Nicky was rather less in favour of deportation than he had been at first, But he seemed favourable to a consultation between the ambassadors of the powers and their respective governments as to what could be done. Then, if we agreed to inform the Sultan of our decision and he refused, we must make him do so by force.'

A second tea at the 'Dantzig' should have offered the Tsar a reprieve. As he wrote: 'We took a walk and then rode up to the forest cottage "Danzig" where we had tea.' But during the return carriage ride, the Queen couldn't resist another grilling. As she reported: 'Alicky and Nicky drove home with me and I talked a little about politics and what Lord Salisbury had said to him.' His account was clipped: 'We went home with Granny.'

Nicky found all these discussions too much. The Tsarina's sister, Victoria, remembered him complaining about his burdensome role as an autocrat. He had been talking enviously to her ever-receptive brother, Ernie: 'I watched Nicky once at a luncheon saying to Ernie how he envied his being a constitutional monarch on whom the blame for all the mistakes made by his ministers was not heaped. Under other circumstances, Nicky would have made a remarkably good constitutional sovereign, for he was in no way narrow-minded nor obsessed by his high position.'

That evening Nicky was laid low with one of his frequent tooth-aches. As he complained in his diary: 'I had an attack of neuralgia.'

Wednesday 30th September
Queen Victoria's diary: 'A little threatening... started with Nicky and Alicky for Mar Lodge'.

In the morning, the Tsar's neuralgia had really set in: 'As a result of the pain, my left cheek swelled up in ugly fashion and I was completely unable to sleep during the night. I cannot bear to show myself in this condition. I stayed home in the morning.' The Tsar had a dread of dentists and several of his teeth rotted early. He finally agreed to see the Queen's physician, Dr. James Reid, who found an infection at the root of a decayed left molar. Dr. Reid prescribed iodine, to be applied at regular intervals throughout the day.

The issue of the Tsar's teeth was raised again only recently, during the ongoing investigations conducted by the Russian orthodox church into the identification of the Romanov bodies. A dental expert was obliged to explain why the Tsarina had had exquisite dental treatment while the Tsar appeared to have had none. 'Nicholas II was like a real Russian peasant. When he had a tooth-ache, he did not have dental treatment, he waited until it was unbearable, drank 100g of vodka, and had his tooth torn out.'

While not ready to expose his cheek on a hunt with the uncles, the Tsar gamely agreed to visit his Aunt Alexandra, at Mar Lodge. He would not have known that, as he passed through the village of Braemar in an open-top carriage, he would be 'showing himself' to a small crowd of cheering well-wishers.

The Tsar made a particular mention of Mar Lodge's modest proportions. In fact the lodge, like Victoria's 'little house', Elm Grove, was quite substantial: 'At 12pm I went off with Granny and Alix to Mar Lodge to Louise and Macduff. They met up with their people – 80 of them with a green flag… We looked over their not very large home and annex, built adjoining the house, in which Aunt Alix… [is] staying. We returned home at 6pm and had tea with Granny.'

After tea, a beleaguered Nicky probably retired to his rooms to nurse his tooth, while Alix showed the Queen her jewellery. Granny's appreciation had a slightly grim edge: 'Alix showed me her beautiful jewels, of which she has quantities, all her own property.'

Lady Lytton retained a seating plan for that night's dinner. She was at the opposite end of the table from the

Tsarina, and sitting between Sir Arthur Bigge and Lady Bigge: wry references to the Russian occupation would obviously have been avoided. The Queen was at the head, with Alix to her right. There was just one untitled diner: Nicky's secretary, Monsieur Dubreuil Eschappar. The Tsar himself was absent. As he recorded disconsolately: 'I had supper alone at 8pm due to my cheek.' There was a sympathetic echo from Granny: 'Nicky didn't dine on account of having a swollen face.'

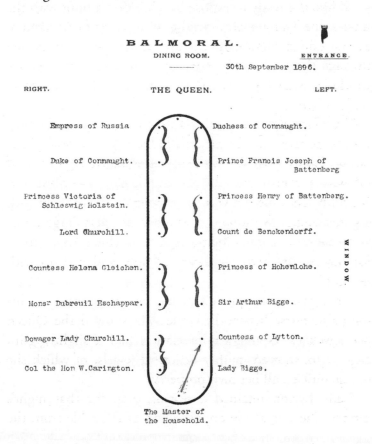

BALMORAL.

DINING ROOM.   ENTRANCE.

30th September 1896.

RIGHT.   THE QUEEN.   LEFT.

Empress of Russia	Duchess of Connaught.
Duke of Connaught.	Prince Francis Joseph of Battenberg
Princess Victoria of Schleswig Holstein.	Princess Henry of Battenberg.
Lord Churchill.	Count de Benckendorff.
Countess Helena Gleichen.	Princess of Hohenlohe.
Monsr Dubreuil Eschappar.	Sir Arthur Bigge.
Dowager Lady Churchill.	Countess of Lytton.
Col the Hon W.Carington.	Lady Bigge.

WINDOW.

The Master of
the Household.

The Tsarina would have been immensely sympathetic; just ten days previously, she had been the one bed-bound, with a headache. Nicky and Alix loved tending each other through life's skirmishes. Following their idyll at 'Walton', the betrothed couple had transferred to Windsor, where Nicky had to be rescued by Alix after locking himself in the lavatory. As he reported: 'Instead of quietly reading the newspapers, I happened to have locked myself accidentally in the bathroom, from which I could in no way extricate myself for more than half an hour. Alix finally managed to open the door from the outside, though I was yelling long and loudly, trying to open it myself, since I had the key.' Two days later, he was complaining of an attack of neuralgia: 'scribbling to you in by no means a merry mood'!

A week later, Nicky was the one offering sympathy as it turned out that his fiancée had not quite shaken off her bout of sciatica. 'Dear Alix is still not able to go out riding with us, since she has just recently finished her medical treatments, but the pain in her legs has still not passed.'

If Alix could not help Nicky directly, she would annotate his diary with chivvying tips. Three days before her young fiancé left for Russia, she gushed: 'My own boysy boysy dear, never changing, always true. Have confidence in your girly dear who loves you more deeply and devotedly than she can ever say.' Nicky never quite matched her 'sweety mannikins' and 'bad boysie'. He concluded his entry for that day with: 'For dinner – Yakov Ivanovich [the priest] and Mr Heath [the English tutor]. Alix sat in my room.'

Thursday 1st October
The Queen hailed: 'A beautiful day'.

The Tsar's ninth day at Balmoral would have been one of his best – his tooth was on the mend and the weather was good: 'I felt great and the swelling has almost gone. The weather remained completely fine and warm.' The Queen joined the chorus: 'Nicky breakfasted with us and was much better.'

The departure of both Salisbury and Uncle Bertie was a further boon. His uncle had left Balmoral to watch his horse, Persimmon, at Newmarket. The Queen very much disapproved, repeating her admonishment: *'Il faut payer pour etre prince.'* But Nicky was exuberant, writing to his mother: 'After he left I had an easier time, because I could at least do what I wanted to, and was NOT obliged to go out shooting every day in the cold and rain.'

Nicky had frequently been baffled by his uncle's predilections. Visiting Bertie at Sandringham during his visit in 1894, he had been unimpressed by his fellow 'queer guests', writing: 'Place full of Jews – all men not Jews talking of nothing but horse racing and horse dealing'. He mused to his mother: 'Rather strange. Most of them were horse dealers, amongst others, a Baron Hirsch.' Hirsch, one of the richest men in the world, had launched a charity to help oppressed Russian Jews. The Tsar, known for his anti-Semitism, must have been particularly nonplussed by Hirsch's presence. His mother, Bertie's sister-in-law, shared his bemusement. As he later wrote: 'Mama never understood how Bertie could enjoy having Jews in his house – never received a satisfactory explanation from her sister.'

An outing with Bertie to a horse sale held few attractions for Nicky: 'We entered a huge tent in which 200 farmers were sitting with their families. Lunch was served to them there, which we also had, sitting sort of on a stage at a separate table. The sale of 50 horses took impossibly long.'

At Balmoral, the Tsar would finally be relishing the end in sight. He may once have looked forward to the visit but, after days of sodden hunts, exhausting talks and a bad tooth, he was ready to go. Indeed, he had already embarked on his packing, a full two days before he was due to leave. He wrote: 'I read and started to pack little by little.'

❧

That day's early lunch got in the way and was clearly unwelcome: 'We had lunch at 12.15 – an ungodly hour.' Baby Olga's customary appearance after the meal would, however, have restored his good spirits. It was certainly much appreciated by the Queen: 'The dear, fat, beautiful baby was brought in as usual toward the end of luncheon and sat playing on the floor with Maurice [the five-year-old Prince Maurice of Battenberg].'

The afternoon featured an outing to a new hideaway cottage, at Glen Gelder. The Tsar boasted of walking to a different 'tea house' while the Queen described a drive to: 'Glen Gelder Shiel' (the Scottish word for a stable). When in Scotland, the Queen preferred to use local patois. It was said that, as soon as she crossed the border, she would hand 'woon poond' to a deserving crofter.

Friday 2nd October
Queen Victoria's diary: 'Very windy… and stormy looking'.

Nicky's high spirits showed no sign of flagging. He even regained his appetite for hunting, gamely taking yet more failures in his stride: 'The day remained good throughout, but a genuine storm blew in. After coffee I went "deer-stalking" alone. I went walking the entire day about the hills, woods and marshes. I was growing hungry and as a result did not kill a thing and did not fire one shot. Really annoying! I met Granny and Alix on the way home.' The Queen, in her diary, insisted that the Tsar was actually accompanied by the Duke of Connaught. It may be that Nicky found Uncle Arthur such relaxing company, in comparison with Bertie, that he didn't feel the need to mention him.

The Queen and Alix, meanwhile, defied the stormy-looking weather, to enjoy a morning drive. After lunch, the pair had a second drive, to 'McIntosh's house' for tea.

That evening, the Queen treated herself to a viewing of Olga in her bath: 'Went to see the dear Baby in its [sic] bath. She is a splendid child and so merry and so full of life.' The Tsarina was a great believer in baths, insisting that they were essential for her daughter's physical well-being. Baby Olga, she wrote: 'has a salt bath every morning according to my wish, as I want her to be as strong as possible having to carry such a plump little body'. The Tsar himself joined the throng: 'After my bath I attended little daughter's bath.'

❦

The Tsar was probably still savouring the various baths when he found himself summoned by Granny for what turned out to be their final weighty discussion.

The Queen later deemed this session particularly worthwhile, convincing herself that she and the Tsar were, at last, in agreement on the Sultan. 'Afterwards Nicky came to my room and I had a very satisfactory conversation with him. He is strongly against deposing the Sultan, which he considers would be very risky and I agree, but he does not object to the various ambassadors consulting together and reporting as to what necessary measures should be taken to prevent further massacres. If the Sultan should refuse to agree to what is decided on, then force would have to be employed.'

Having sorted out the Sultan, the pair moved on to the happier topic of presentations. As he put it: 'The two of us sorted out gifts for all of the court here.'

There was a sum of £1,000 to be distributed amongst the staff; the Queen's head gamekeepers and Ballater's stationmaster each received a gold watch. The Tsarina would present the ladies-in-waiting with a sachet of flawless diamonds and pearl jewellery.

Nicky may not have given much thought to security over his stay, but he presented the local police sergeant with a diamond ring. Another policeman on duty received a silver watch and chain, inscribed with the Russian eagle. The wife of the chief officer of the Queen's household police was given a gold bracelet.

Dr. Reid was awarded a gold cigarette case with an

imperial crest studded with diamonds. Presenting the cigarette case later, in the castle library, the grateful Tsar was
brimming with goodwill, even assuring Reid that he had
his heart set on returning to Balmoral next year.

The Queen was gratified by Nicky's responses as she pressed
him for information about his forthcoming trip to France:
'With regard to my remark on Russia's present great inti-
macy with France, Nicky told me that, finding herself
isolated, owing to the Triple Alliance [between Germany,
Austria-Hungary and Italy] which was formed behind
her [Russia's] back, she formed an alliance or treaty with
France, but purely military and defensive.'

She added later: 'Nicky did not seem at all to relish the
French and regretted the visit to Paris, which was unavoidable. I said it was so important that Russia and England
should go well together, as they were the most powerful
empires, for then the world must be at peace.' The day after
the Romanovs' departure, Georgie wrote a letter to his
grandmother in which he revealed his own distaste for the
French enterprise: 'I trust their tiresome visit to Paris will
pass off satisfactorily.'

With all his worries about political conversations, Nicky
was proud of his rapport with the Queen. During his stay
two years earlier, when he had become engaged to Alix,
he had refused a dinner invitation to the guards' mess at

Windsor: 'because Granny loves me so and doesn't like me missing dinner'. The happy bond continued to flourish, despite the young Tsarevich finding himself embroiled in arduous diplomatic duties, not least receiving Russian trade companies and entertaining the formidable, exiled French Empress Eugenie. He kept a stiff record of his efforts: 'We had dinner at 9pm – I sat next to the Empress... They sang selected melodies from the new opera *Signa* – very weak colourless music by the English composer Cowen [Sir Frederic Hymen Cowen]... My shoes were hurting my feet terribly.'

The Queen, smitten in her turn, was soon enjoying impromptu greetings from Russian sailors: 'Tea all together in the upper alcove and afterwards all the Russian sailors from *Polar Star* [the Dowager's yacht] came up on the terrace after having walked about in the grounds. They drew up and I bowed to them, all calling out a greeting in Russian. Nicky then told them I was pleased to see them and they answered and then marched off. They were fine looking, tall men.'

In a letter to his brother, Nicky had given a jubilant description of their burgeoning relationship, comparing himself to the Queen's closest companions, Mr Brown (who had died 12 years before) and the Munshi: 'It seems funny to me, all this life here and the extent to which I have become part of the English family. I have become almost as indispensable to my future grandmother as her two Indians and her Scotsman.' The second Indian he referred to was Mohammed Bukhsh.

It seemed the only fault the Queen could ever find with her prospective 'grandson' was his over-generosity. During that same sojourn in England in 1894, Nicky and Alix had spent their last day together visiting the Main Street at West Cowes. Nicky wrote: 'We rode by to a store where they make enamelled flags for pins and brooches and ordered two little ones for Alix.'

The brooches would follow lavish engagement presents, not least a Fabergé sautoir of pearls valued at $175,000. Parting gifts included a diamond brooch bearing the romantic inscription: 'Nicky's goodbye tear'. Examining the gifts, the Queen issued a solemn warning to her grand-daughter: 'Don't get too proud.'

After playing host to the betrothed couple, the Queen would always consider herself part of their charmed union. Before he left, Nicky had been full of warmth towards Granny. She described him, in her curious English: 'thanking me much for all my kindness and kissing me affectionately'. He referred only briefly to his impending departure: 'I spent the last evening with my fiancée!' Between 'evening' and 'with', Alix added one of her starker messages: 'Ever true and ever loving, faithful pure and strong as death.'

Four months later, when Nicky and Alix were married in the Winter Palace, in St Petersburg, the Queen held a celebratory dinner for 37 guests at Windsor Castle. 'Her Majesty's Dinner' featured 'Escalope de Turbot à la Crème, La Mousse de Faisans and Le Boeuf à la Mode. An ornate menu gave the date as 'Monday, 26th November, 1894', though in Russia it would, of course, have been 14th November. The Queen offered a toast: 'I propose the health of their majesties the Emperor and Empress of Russia, my dear grandchildren.'

Nicholas and Alexandra on their wedding day, November 1894

...and as depicted in a painting of the ceremony at the
Winter Palace in St Petersburg

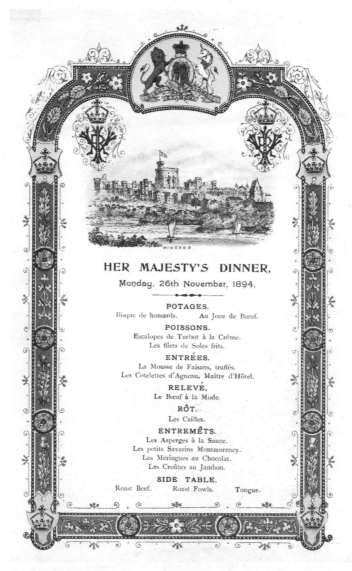

HER MAJESTY'S DINNER,

Monday, 26th November, 1894.

POTAGES.
Bisque de homards.   Au Joue de Bœuf.

POISSONS.
Escalopes de Turbot à la Crême.
Les filets de Soles frits.

ENTRÉES.
La Mousse de Faisans, truffés.
Les Cotelettes d'Agneau, Maître d'Hôtel.

RELEVÉ,
Le Bœuf à la Mode.

RÔT.
Les Cailles.

ENTREMÊTS.
Les Asperges à la Sauce.
Les petits Savarins Montmorency.
Les Meringues au Chocolat.
Les Croûtes au Jambon.

SIDE TABLE.
Roast Beef.   Roast Fowls.   Tongue.

The menu for Queen Victoria's celebratory dinner at
Windsor Castle

Saturday 3rd October
Queen Victoria's diary: 'Showery and dark... Nicky and Alicky breakfasted with us.'

During the imperial couple's last morning at Balmoral, the photographers, W. and D. Downey, returned to film moving pictures. The shoot took place outside the main entrance and the images can now be seen on the internet. The Queen is being pulled along in a buggy, awkwardly holding a lively little white dog. The Tsar and Tsarina walk alongside: Nicky looks self-conscious, walking stiffly and brandishing a cane. Towards the end of the reel, there are glimpses of the ubiquitous Munshi. In one of the stills, the Tsarina stands behind the buggy, gazing at the Duke of Connaught, now wearing a kilt.

Nicky would have been thankful not to be wearing a kilt. He had once worn one and not enjoyed the experience: 'I never before exposed my knees.'

He had also successfully jettisoned the Scots Greys uniform. His choice of conventional dress, however, did him few favours. Though he is one of the few looking square on, his appearance is less tsar than diminutive bank manager. No one smiles.

The Tsar was strangely unexcited by the shoot: 'After coffee we went outside together into the garden, where they took our picture, both stills and moving pictures.' The Queen was a little more expansive: 'At 12 went down to below the terrace, near the ball room and were photographed by Downey by the new cinematic process, which makes moving pictures by winding off a reel of films. We were walking up and down and the children jumping

British and Russian royals, including the Duke of Connaught,
the Tsar, Queen Victoria and the Tsarina

about. Then took a turn in the pony chair and not far from the garden cottage.'

Nearly two months later, the Queen did seem moved, or at least intrigued, after watching a screening at Windsor. The film marked the first time a British monarch had been captured on a motion picture: 'After tea went to the Red drawing room where so-called "animated pictures" were shown off, including the groups taken in September [in fact October] at Balmoral. It is a very wonderful process, representing people, their movements and action, as if they were alive.'

On that last afternoon the imperial couple marked their visit in a more traditional way: As the Queen recorded:

'Then took a turn in the pony chair, and not far from the garden cottage, Nicky and Alicky each planted a tree.' John Mitchie, the head forester at Balmoral, had selected two Cumbrian pines. He was obliged to guide Nicky through the process of filling in the base around the trees with soil. The Tsar makes no mention in his diary of the planting or his confusion: 'We went for a walk with Granny. We had lunch with all of Beatrice's children, on the occasion of her younger son's [Maurice's] birthday. At 3.30 Aunt Alix [Bertie's wife] arrived with our girl cousins. We did not see them long, since we had to go off soon with Granny.'

The Queen made another of her rare allusions to her feelings, referring to Nicky and Alicky's imminent departure: 'In the afternoon drove out with them, alas!, for the last time and went to Invercauld and back by the Balloch Bhui. It was rather showery and dark.' The Tsar, clearly by now inured to showers and darkness, mentioned nothing of the conditions. He wrote: 'We had tea with her [the Queen] at home,' adding, 'I changed into my "Scots Greys" frock coat. Dinner at 8.45.'

In a recreation of the arrival ceremony, kilted Scottish attendants lit the Romanovs' way from the castle with blazing torches. After their departure, the Queen referred, again, to her sadness: 'At 10 dear Nicky and Alicky left to my great regret as I am so fond of them both… Went to the door to see our dear visitors leave. There were again the Highlanders bearing torches, but no pipes.' Whatever the Tsar told Dr. Reid about his hopes to return, he seemed to journey on without a backward glance: 'Around 10pm we bid farewell to Balmoral under torchlight and with the same convoy we went to Ballater.'

The couple took an overnight train for Portsmouth. *The Times* gave another exhaustively detailed description of the Tsarina's outfit. She wore: 'a pink silk dress with a train, heli otrope-coloured travelling cloak and cape with white lace, trimmed with white fur at the throat'. This was topped by a 'small bonnet to match the cape, decorated with heliotrope, white and light-blue coloured flowers'. The *Graphic* was in agreement: 'Another long railway voyage was set forth upon in a light pink silk gown and a heliotrope mantle and white bonnet.'

Little Olga's night-time farewell was very different from her glittering arrival. There was just a short reference to her tearful upset, as she was whisked off by her nanny to a sort of nursery carriage. As *The Times* reported: 'The child was inconsolable at her mother's departure, and was carried weeping into her sleeping chamber.'

The Tsar's account of the subsequent journey south is characteristically sparse: 'We boarded the train and at 11pm we were under way. Alix and I were in Granny's comfortable wagon-car. We slept in one section.' As he gained distance from Scotland, his spirits seemed to lift, despite the continuing bad weather: 'We slept beautifully… At 8.45 we stopped in Preston for coffee. It was raining and cold. We had lunch in Oxford at 2pm and saw there the former bombastic governor "Lord Harris". At 5.30 we arrived at Portsmouth. There were two honour guards – the heavy artillery and seamen.'

There was no mention of security. Did the Tsar think

back to the note he had written to Lynedoch Gardiner explaining that he couldn't possibly visit London and that he would have to travel straight to Portsmouth? There is certainly a note of relief in the Queen's diary: 'Heard Nicky and Alicky had reached Preston safely.'

The Tsar continued: 'Directly upon getting off the train, we boarded the *Polar Star*. The *Standart* stood in the road-stead.' The *Polar Star* belonged to the Tsar's mother, the Dowager Empress.

A photograph exists of the exotically named Sir Hamnet Holditch Share, later gentleman usher to King George V, on the *Osborne*, 'on the day of Emperor of Russia leaving'. Sir Hamnet is looking away from the camera and out to sea, perhaps anxious about the proceedings. In 1932 he wrote his memoir, *Under Great Bear and Southern Cross: Fifty Years Afloat and Ashore*. He retained, alongside this picture of himself, a photograph of the *Standart* at Portsmouth.

That evening, still moored in Portsmouth Harbour, the Tsar was jubilant as he found himself enjoying Russian culture once again: 'At 8 o'clock we had dinner with the English admirals, generals and our suite. We visited the *Victoria and Albert*, on which Uncle Arthur, Aunt Lonischen and Helena are spending the night. At last they listened to our music at dinner.'

⚜

Georgie later assured his grandmother: 'I know they were charmed by their visit to Balmoral.' In fact the Queen later admitted that, for all her first happy impressions, she felt Alix had become a little aloof. She had apparently, at one

The *Standart*, in Portsmouth Harbour, to which the Tsar
returned delightedly after the rigours of Balmoral

Sir Hamnet Holditch Share, later gentleman usher to
King George V, on the *Osborne*, 'on the day of
Emperor of Russia leaving'

point, even been driven to talk to her about the importance of smiling and appearing pleasant. She would, additionally, have been conscious that, despite her immediate satisfaction with that last session, her talks with Nicky had been inconclusive. The author and historian, E.F. Benson, wrote: 'Neither she [the Queen], nor England, nor Lord Salisbury knew any more about his real sentiment towards England than if he had never been to Balmoral at all.' It was Benson's brother A.C. Benson who later edited Queen Victoria's letters.

⁂

The somewhat muted visit to chilly, wet Balmoral was thrown into the shade by the dazzling success of the Romanovs' subsequent five days in Paris. Preparations for the decorations had begun almost a fortnight before, as platforms were built, with crimson and gilt fringes and flagstaffs. The front of the Bourbon Palace was cleaned and the inscriptions re-gilded; chestnut trees along the Champs-Elysées were decorated with red and white paper roses, at a cost of 500 francs per tree.

Royal guests had not been entertained since 1867 and more than 900,000 spectators lined the streets of Paris to watch the open landaus, chanting: 'Long live the Tsar.' Nicky was overwhelmed: 'I can only compare it with my entry into Moscow [for the Coronation].'

Hundreds of boats gathered on the Seine, festooned with French and Russian flags. During elaborate firework displays, the Eiffel Tower was engulfed in cascades of flames and the Place de la Concorde was, according to an over-enthusiastic *Times*: 'literally ablaze with light'.

It was reported that security was dealt with quietly and efficiently. Suspected terrorists had been detained or turned away from Paris. Routes were selected according to how easily they could be policed; at one point 32,000 soldiers stood in double lines along the streets.

The French paid tribute to the Tsar's 'graceful figure, serious countenance and erect bearing' not to mention his 'easy mastery' of his horse. The baby, Grand Duchess Olga, was helped to wave at admirers chanting: 'Vive la bébé' and 'La tsarinette'. The crowds snapped up Russian teddy bears, sweets decorated with Russian flags and soup labelled 'Le Tsar'. A polka was composed 'pour la Grand Duchess Olga'.

The Tsarina was included in the craze: portraits of all three Romanovs appeared on items of tableware. But she was the least fêted. She had been looking forward to this first trip to Paris, thrilled to be staying in the rooms of one of her heroines: the ill-fated Marie-Antoinette. Her shyness, however, was, by this time, compounded by the worst symptoms of early pregnancy. She felt tired and nauseous, disinclined to socialise. She unwittingly caused offence by refusing to meet grand dames with ties to the old monarchy. She could never quite grasp the French idea of embracing both old and new regimes.

❧

Queen Victoria wrote to Nicky with strict instructions: 'Kindly use your influence and let the French understand that you do not intend to support them in their constant inimicality towards England, which is the cause of much annoyance and difficulty to us… I would not have written this had you not told me that the agreement, or alliance or whatever it is called, is ONLY of a military nature.'

But Nicky, now a safe distance from Balmoral, was basking in the glow of a new French-Russian accord, proudly presenting the Minister of War, Jean Baptiste Billot, with a portrait set in diamonds. *The Times* deemed the portrait: 'The highest mark of personal distinction which the Russian Emperor has at his disposal for a person not of supreme rank'. It was a curious situation, as the historian Robert K. Massie acknowledged: 'Diplomacy made military allies of Europe's greatest republic and its most absolute autocracy.'

Fortified by his bullish mood, Nicky now informed Granny that he had not broached any subject connected with 'inimicality', before adding loftily: 'Politics, alas, are not the same as private or domestic affairs and they are not guided by personal or relationship feeling. History is one's real positive teacher in these matters and for me personally, except that I have always got the sacred example of my beloved father and also the result and proof of all his deeds.' The Queen would not have appreciated Nicky's effusive tribute to his 'barbaric, Asiatic and tyrannical' father.

The flow of chatty family letters fell to a dribble, though Nicky never quite gave up his fond conclusions, writing on 3rd November: 'Now, goodbye, dearest Grandmama, with my best love to all, believe me your most loving and devoted grandson Nicky.'

Nearly four and a half years after the Romanovs' visit to Balmoral, Queen Victoria died, at Osborne, in January 1901.

The Tsarina was devastated by the news of her grandmother's death, writing to her sister Victoria: 'I cannot really believe she has gone, that we shall never see her any more. Since one can remember, she was in our life and a dearer kinder being never was.' By then pregnant with her fourth daughter, Anastasia, Alix could not travel to Windsor for the funeral. Instead, she and her sister Ella, wife of the Russian Grand Duke Serge, attended a memorial service in St Petersburg. The Tsarina and the Grand Duchess both wept openly for their grandmother. The Tsarina's tears may have come as a surprise to the Russians, who had always dismissed her as cold and haughty: sadly for her, the demonstration was already too late.

The sorrowful conclusion of Alix's letter to Madgie, written at the end of her visit to Balmoral, had proven strangely prescient. 'It has been such a very short stay and I leave dear kind grandmama with a heavy heart. Who knows when we may meet again and where.'

Nicky wrote a sympathetic letter to Uncle Bertie, stressing his high hopes for continuing goodwill between the Russians and the British. He described how 'at home' he had felt in Britain: 'She [the Queen] was so remarkably kind and touching towards me since the first time I ever saw her... I felt quite at home when I lived at Windsor and later in Scotland... I am quite sure that with your help, dear Bertie, the friendly relations between our two countries shall become still closer than in the past, notwithstanding occasional slight frictions in the Far East. May the new century bring England and Russia together for their mutual interests and for the general peace of the world.'

With all Nicky's and Uncle Bertie's good intentions, Anglo-Russian relations would be sorely tested over the next few years. At one point, the Tsar, doubtless prompted by one of his ministers, decided to write to his uncle criticising Britain's role in the Boer War. The war had begun before Victoria's death and ended in 1902: 'A small people are desperately defending their country, a part of their land is devastated, their families locked together in camps, their farms burnt... it looks more like a war of extermination.' Bertie beat down his timorous nephew, raging against an: 'incessant storm of obloquy and misrepresentation which has been directed against England from every part of the continent... I do not know whether you are aware that the war was begun... by the Boers and was unprovoked by any single act, on the part of England, of which the Boers, according to international law, had any right to complain.' There was no reply.

Though this early skirmish was swiftly resolved, it exposed ominous fissures in the relationship between the new King and the Tsar, not least a disparity in their authority. Writing his ill-judged letter, Nicky seems to have forgotten just how sharp his uncle could be. It could additionally have been argued that he was in no position to be speaking up for the little guy.

In April 1902, Vladimir Ilyich Lenin selected London as the best place to print and distribute his subversive pamphlet,

Iskra (*Spark*). Seventeen issues were duly published under the auspices of one of Britain's pioneering marxists, Harry Quelch, who ran a printing press in Clerkenwell Green: the building still exists as the Marx Memorial Library.

Lenin and his wife, Krupskaya, lived in London for just over a year, in Holford Square, Pentonville. They took pains to cover their tracks, living under aliases, as Mr and Mrs Richter, and employing invisible ink and elaborate code words in their correspondence. These code words included 'handkerchiefs' for passports while 'brewing beer' and 'warm fur' served for the titles of various illegal books.

The 'Richters' may have been paranoid about security, but they were also determined to see the sights. Or, as Krupskaya wrote: 'We began to look around this citadel of capitalism with curiosity.' Lenin took a particular shine to the Reading Room of the British Museum, writing to the director to ask for access, claiming he: 'came from Russia to study the land question'. He included a reference from a Mr Mitchell and closed his letter with: 'Believe me, Sir, to be yours faithfully, Jacob Richter.'

There were visits to Regents Park Zoo and expeditions to the country. As Lenin wrote: 'Nadia [Krupskaya] and I have often been out locally in search of "real countryside" and have found it.' After Krupskaya's mother arrived, the trio enjoyed a picnic. 'We took sandwiches with us instead of lunch,' Lenin wrote, 'and spent the whole of one Sunday "ins grune" ["in the countryside"]... We are the only people among the comrades here who are exploring every bit of the surrounding country.'

The only low point seems to have been the English food: as Krupskaya complained, 'We found that all those ox-tails, skates fried in fat and indigestible cakes were not made for Russian stomachs.'

It was during these months that Lenin first met Leon Trotsky, at the couple's flat. Lenin had summoned him from his Siberian exile and Trotsky duly arrived at dawn, one morning of October 1902. He spoke no English and carried virtually nothing but Lenin's address scribbled on a piece of paper. He appeared at the couple's front door, having successfully commandeered a cab: Krupskaya paid the fare.

Trotsky later recalled Lenin giving him a tour of the London sights, highlighting 'their' (the capitalists') Westminster Abbey. The pair may well have visited the Old Red Lion Pub in Islington, where various Communist factions would meet upstairs; Lenin would sometimes ask the landlord to remove the pub's dumb waiter so that he could listen in from a safe distance below.

In 1903, following pogroms in Russia, there were protests in London against the Tsar. It was claimed that the anti-Semitic Tsar had encouraged the pogroms, then delayed taking steps to restore order. During two days of turmoil, 49 Jews were killed and hundreds injured. Protesters marched from Mile End to a rally in Hyde Park, where the aristocratic Russian revolutionary Prince Kropotkin gave speeches and was held aloft by the crowd.

Meanwhile, from early 1904 to late 1905, Russia was embroiled in a war against Japan. This, too, created problems between Russia and Britain, as the British sided with the Japanese. Indeed Britain was sometimes criticised by the Russians for promoting the original hostilities.

In October 1904, in what became known as the Dogger

Bank incident, the Russian fleet opened fire on British trawlers in the North Sea. Disoriented in the fog, they had mistaken the boats for enemy vessels, and killed three British sailors. The King was eventually obliged to weigh in, calming British politicians and extracting an agreement from Russia to pay compensation. The Liberal politician, Charles Carrington, who had given such a vivid description of Bertie in his Russian uniform, later paid tribute to the King's skilful manoeuvres, recalling: 'the anxious time he [Bertie] went through, over the Russian shelling of our fishing fleet. He saw at once that it was a mistake and not a question of war; but he seems to have had a good deal of trouble in keeping ministers quiet.'

The war had consequences at the imperial court, as one of the English nurses refused to toe the Russian party line. The Tsarina had taken on the 36-year-old Miss Eager in 1899, to look after her new-born third daughter, Maria. An Irish Protestant, Margaretta Eager was immediately captivated by the orthodox rituals, particularly the baby's christening. Little Maria was dipped in the font three times, she wrote, after which: 'the hair was cut in four places in the form of a cross. What was cut off was rolled in wax and thrown into the font... according to Russian superstition the good or evil future of the child's life depends on whether the hair sinks or swims.' She described her relief as the auguries went well: 'Maria's hair... all sank at once, so there is no need for alarm concerning her future.'

The new English nurse was 'mad about politics', noted the Tsar's disapproving sister, Olga: along with the Irish Orchie, Miss Eager was normally referred to as English. The nanny's obsession with the Crimean War created no difficulties. The Tsar and Tsarina may not have appreciated Granny's Crimean War trophies, but they were content to let Miss Eager visit graves at Sevastopol. As she wrote: 'We passed through the famous quarries where the English lay entrenched and so much desperate fighting took place.'

Nor were there objections to Miss Eager's further fixation with the more recent Dreyfus case; though the Tsar's sister Olga recalled one dramatic lapse, when her obsession overtook her sense of responsibility: 'Once she even forgot that Maria was in her bath, and started discussing the [Dreyfus] case with a friend. Maria, naked and dripping, scrambled out of the bath and started running up and down the palace corridor. Fortunately I arrived just at that moment, picked her up, and carried her back to Miss Eager, who was still talking about Dreyfus!'

The real difficulties began when the nanny started taking the Japanese side against the Russians. She was horrified to hear the four-year-old Maria berating 'horrid little people' who 'destroyed our poor little ships and drowned our sailors.' As Miss Eager wrote, it was: 'very sad to witness the wrathful, vindictive spirit that the war raised in my little charges'. She instructed all four Grand Duchesses to stop cursing the Japanese. Olga, now eight years old, was suitably chastened : 'I didn't know that the Japs were people like ourselves. I thought they were only like monkeys.'

This sort of subversion of the official line could not be allowed to continue; in October 1904, Miss Eager was fired. The birth of the Tsarevich, Alexis, four months previously, had brought the issue to a head. That Miss Eager might corrupt the little Grand Duchesses was bad enough; but it was unthinkable that she might influence a future tsar.

Nicky wrote in his diary: 'After many weeks of wavering Alix, strongly supported by myself and Princess Galitzine, at last decided to dismiss the Englishwoman, the children's nurse Miss Eager... this has caused trouble and dissension enough.'

Always claiming she left of her own volition, for 'private and personal reasons', Miss Eager was horrified to read British press reports of an English nurse dismissed for stealing papers from the Tsar's study. She wrote furiously to *The Times*: 'I now write, as I am the only English nurse who has lately left Russia, to emphatically deny the truth

Miss Eager (on the left) and Orchie (in black, on the right) with a nursery maid and three of the little Grand Duchesses in 1900

of the story... so far from being ignominiously dismissed, I received from the Empress a handsome money present, and a pension for my life was settled upon me. At Christmas I was the recipient of letters, cards and gifts from the Empress and the imperial children.'

Miss Eager's nursing credentials were not in question and she had definitely retained the affection of at least some of her charges. But her portrayal of herself as a favourite of the Empress was stretching the truth, as, of course, was her claim to be English: she was born in Limerick, the daughter of a prison governor.

Incidentally, the first Miss Coster, who was still working for the Tsar's sister, Xenia, did not share Miss Eager's sympathies for the Japanese. Her seven charges never forgot her endless threats to 'get the Japs' on to them.

Two years after Miss Eager's departure, Orchie also returned to England, where she died and was buried in Forest Gate, Essex. The Tsarina was sorrowful but philosophical: 'I miss my dear old Orchie so much, as you can imagine. But her sufferings are over now and one could not wish it otherwise.'

In her will, Orchie left 'Nana', the English nurse of the Tsar's sister Olga, an easy chair.

❧

In 1905, London was selected as the venue for the first Bolshevik congress. Fifty delegates spoke at different locations over four weeks, including Anatoly Lunacharsky, the future Soviet commissar of enlightenment. The congress was held four months after Bloody Sunday, during which the Tsar's soldiers killed or wounded 1,000 peaceful demonstrators in St Petersburg. After the killings, newspaper reporters had besieged Prince Kropotkin's house in

Bromley, hoping for an interview. He was ill and refused to come to the door, eventually sending out a note saying: 'Down with the Romanovs!'

True to British form, visiting speakers at the congress had no fear of being interrupted on security grounds. When supporters of the Russian Social Democrat Labour Party, RSDLP, gathered at the premises of a Communist club, at 107 Charlotte Street, nobody seems to have questioned their claim to be members of an angling club. At one point, a police detective was ordered to eavesdrop on a meeting of anarchists at the Crown and Woolpack pub, in St John Street. He successfully hid in a cupboard, but found himself unable to pass on any information. As he reported: 'The meeting was conducted all in Russian and I know nothing of this language so am unable to report the subjects they discussed.' At some point, during 1905, Lenin was attacked by a mob during a lecture. In the ensuing confusion, he was rescued by Special Branch officers who assumed he was a police spy.

The following year, in the summer of 1906, the Tsar sought a return visit from the British royals. The reasons behind the invitation were not entirely straightforward. Russia needed to stabilise her finances by borrowing money, and the Prime Minister, Count Sergei Witte, believed that banks would be more inclined to lend if they felt Russia was on friendly terms with Britain. Bertie recognised the ploy and didn't like it: 'Witte's object is that by my going I should enable him to float a loan. What an extraordinary idea! And one that does not appeal to me in any way...'

Indeed, at this particular point, Bertie was not inclined to agree to any sort of meeting with his nephew. The Dogger Bank incident and the Russo-Japanese conflict had created difficulties between the two countries. But the main problem had been Russian's ongoing political turmoil. Outbreaks of violence would continue up to the inauguration of Russia's first parliament, the Duma, towards the end of 1906.

The King wrote a letter explaining his reluctance, comparing himself favourably to the German Kaiser: 'I honestly confess that I can see no particular object in visiting the Emperor in Russia this year. The country is in a very unsettled state and will, I fear, not improve for some time to come. I hardly think that the country at home [England] would much approve of my going there for a while. I have no desire to play the part of the German Emperor, who always meddles in other people's business. What advice could I possibly give the [Russian] Emperor as to the management of his country? What right have I to do so, even if he were to listen to me, which I much doubt...'

There was a broader feeling, among government officials, that a Russo-British meeting could prove politically expedient. But Bertie was not to be swayed, at that point, even by his Foreign Secretary, Sir Edward Grey. Six days after the King had written, Grey wrote to the King's private secretary insisting that, if there was no more bloodshed inside Russia, the King should agree to a meeting in the Baltic: 'An entente with Russia... is the thing most to be desired in our foreign policy. It will complete and strengthen the entente with France and add very much to the comfort and strength of our position. But it all depends upon the Tsar and he depends on the King.'

There had been awkwardnesses on both sides. The Tsar had, on one occasion recently, vetoed a visit that the Royal Navy was due to pay to Kronstadt. He had been worried, not least, by the prospect of 'free' English sailors mixing with his own restless fleet.

However, in autumn 1906, the King showed a change of heart. Curiously, this seems to have been brought about by his fascination with Russia's charismatic Foreign Minister, Alexander Izvolsky. In October 1906, he sent an urgent telegraph to the permanent under secretary at the Foreign Office, Sir Charles Hardinge: 'The great Izvolsky is at Paris… I would give anything to see him.'

The great Izvolsky, then aged 50, was known for his stylishly curled moustaches, lorgnette and white spats. He was described by Robert K. Massie as: 'an archetype of the Old World professional diplomat. A plumpish, dandified man, he wore a pearl pin in his white waistcoat… and always trailed a faint touch of violet eau de cologne.'

Izvolsky, equally keen to meet the King, rushed, forthwith, to Buckingham Palace. Charles Hardinge later paid tribute to the pair's contribution towards creating an entente. He insisted that they: 'helped materially to smooth the path of the negotiations then in progress for an agreement with Russia'.

The culmination of these negotiations was the signing of an Anglo-Russian agreement, on 31st August 1907. The convention that the British Ambassador, Sir Arthur Nicolson, put forward had nothing to do with Europe. But it indicated a rapprochement and was a sign to Europe that Russia was moving forward under an Anglo-French banner. The King took no part in the actual drafting of the agreement, but he was kept informed of the details and gave regular signals of approval.

❧❧❧

That same year, Joseph Stalin came to London for an RSDLP congress, chaired by a full 300 delegates. Meetings were held at the Brotherton Church on Southgate Road, and the Socialist Club, on Fulbourne Street, Whitechapel. Lenin returned to London for the congress, taking another participant, Maxim Gorky, on a tour of his beloved British Museum. He would have been glad of the opportunity to prise Gorky away from his rooms at the Imperial Hotel, Russell Square. He was convinced that his comrade's health was being compromised by the hotel's damp.

After leaving London, Lenin made frequent return trips. In May 1908, he was lodging, briefly, at 21 Tavistock Place while working at the British Library, carrying out research for his book: *Materialism and Empirio-Criticism*.

Kropotkin never lost his negative view of British politics, retaining his: 'conviction that a revolution was impossible in England'. Lenin expressed similar doubts to Trotsky: 'The English proletariat has in itself many revolutionary and Socialist elements but they are all mixed up with conservatism, with religion and prejudices, and there seems to be no way in which these elements can come to the top.'

But up to 25,000 protesters had attended the demonstration against the pogrom in 1903, and Socialist churches in England were definitely in the ascendant. In 1908, there were about 50 such churches, each with 300 to 500 congregants. At one point, Lenin took Trotsky to a Socialist church service, probably at the Seven Sisters Church, on the Seven Sisters Road. According to Trotsky the congregation sang: 'Almighty God, put an end to all kings and rich men.'

REVAL

If God heard the Socialists' prayers, He showed little sign of responding. In June 1908 Tsar Nicholas met Edward VII at Reval (now Tallinn), the first visit of a British sovereign to Russia. Kings and rich men were in abundance and most were, apparently, in good health.

King Edward's journey to meet the Tsar at Reval, June 1908. The visit caused protest in Parliament, which had been horrified by the massacre at the Winter Palace and the Tsar's dismissal of the Duma.

The route to Reval

The meeting was intended to be an informal, family affair, adding a final flourish to the Anglo-Russian agreement of the previous year. King Edward VII would be accompanied by Queen Alexandra and their daughter Victoria, by then aged 40.

The Tsar, also 40, would be with the 36-year-old Tsarina and all five of their children. Little Olga was now a slim 12-year-old; beyond the broad, Slavic brow so admired by Lady Lytton, there were few traces of the chubby baby of Balmoral. Her younger sister, Tatiana, aged ten, was tall and slight, with a particularly fine, pretty face. The two elder daughters had rather plaintive expressions, while the third, eight-year-old Maria, was sensual looking with fuller features. The youngest, Anastasia, aged six, had a beguilingly sharp, characterful look, befitting her reputation as the family joker. She gave the impression of being the least biddable. The sisters would be joined by the dark-haired, cherubic three-year-old Tsarevich, Alexis.

The news of the meeting greatly cheered Miss Eager. Three years after leaving the Romanovs, she was successfully running a boarding house in London's Holland Park. But she still nurtured fond memories of the Russian court. She took the opportunity of sending Tatiana an 11th birthday greeting: 'I am so glad that Uncle Bertie, Auntie Alex and Auntie Toria are going over to pay you a visit.'

There was no mention of her favourite subject, politics, but there was a typically bleak addendum: 'Do you know that they [the British royals] passed quite close to my house lately, going to visit the Great Exhibition which has been opened here. And though they did not pass my house, but only the end of the street, I put up flags, and put scarlet bunting with ER and a big gilt crown round my balcony... I wonder did they see it, but I am afraid not.'

The Foreign Secretary, Edward Grey, gave reassurances

concerning the Reval meeting in the House of Commons. He insisted that there were no plans to negotiate any new treaty or convention. He would not even be attending: in his place would be Charles Hardinge, a former Ambassador to Russia.

The president of the Duma gave his approval of Grey's speech. Izvolsky insisted that the Russians, generally, had been impressed by its 'tone of moderation and firmness'. On 2nd June, a British diplomat in St Petersburg, Hugh O'Beirne, wrote with further good news: 'Moderate Liberal politicians ... believe that an increase of English influence can only tend to further the Liberal cause.'

The leader of the Russian cadet party declared that the only objectors to the meeting were: 'on the extreme right of the Duma and the extreme left'. There was, indeed, one party leader who raged that Reval: 'condones the worst deeds of the ruling class'. His fellow objectors, however, seemed to content themselves with thanking their British supporters. These comprised, first, the radicals who put forward a motion protesting against the meeting's classification as a state visit. And, secondly, the Labour MP for Leeds, Mr J. O'Grady.

The Russian press was mostly positive, though O'Beirne admitted that there had been the odd outburst. A week before the meeting, he wrote: 'Papers in this country have been practically unanimous in welcoming the King's visit in terms which for friendliness and cordiality leave nothing to be desired... It seems scarcely worthwhile to notice the utterances of the *Russkaya Znamia* [*The Russian Banner*] which indulges in a virulent attack on Great Britain and her policy. This is the discredited organ of the violently reactionary "Association of the Russian People" and its opinions may be safely neglected.

'Another reactionary paper of little standing, the *Sviet*, displayed a certain amount of coolness in regard to the visit and, referring to the questions asked in Parliament, spoke of the traditional enmity of England.'

He added that two German papers remained sceptical: 'Perhaps I should mention also the two papers issued in St Petersburg in German, the *Petersburger Zeitung* and the *Herold*, [which] make no pretence of feeling gratified at the prospect of the King's arrival... *Herold* protests against "Anglomania raging around it".'

The Tsar was buoyed up after hearing that the meeting had been discussed in the House of Commons. As Izvolsky told Hardinge: 'The Tsar was extremely glad that the debate had taken place, since it had shown to the world that the two great political parties in England shared the same friendly feeling towards Russia, and dissentients, having been free to speak, spoke to say all that they wanted against him and his government, the air had been cleared as after a thunderstorm.'

The Tsar was, once again, wide of the mark. The air was not clear and dissentients at Westminster were growing in number. On 4th June, 59 of the 284 members present cast their votes against the meeting. The Tsar's human rights record was still presenting a problem. Russia's prisons were grossly overcrowded, and beatings, though officially forbidden, were regularly carried out. Death sentences were on the rise: official figures put the numbers sentenced to death between 1906 and 1909 at 2,694.

Ramsay MacDonald now called the Tsar a 'common

murderer' and accused those attending the Reval meeting of 'hobnobbing with a blood-stained killer'. Keir Hardie, the first Labour MP, backed the radicals' motion, protesting against the meeting's classification. He echoed the angry Russian party leader, insisting that the visit was: 'condoning the atrocities perpetrated by the Tsar'.

Feathers continued to be ruffled, as three 'dissentients' found their names removed from a list of guests for the royal garden party at Windsor on 20th June. The MPs were Keir Hardie, Victor Grayson, an independent member, and Arthur Ponsonby, a Liberal. The penalising of Ponsonby was particularly controversial, as he was the brother of Bertie's melancholic-looking assistant private secretary, Sir Frederick (Fritz) Ponsonby.

During the ensuing row, the Liberal Whip, Alexander Murray, warned that the story might be leaked to the press: 'and he [Arthur Ponsonby] will be held up as a martyr to principle, for these Fleet Street scribblers will gloat over his exclusion'. Calm was finally restored after Arthur Ponsonby was induced to apologise and the King to accept the apology. As Bertie wrote: 'I accept Mr A. Ponsonby's explanation and regrets expressed in his letter and look upon the incident as closed.'

The Russian Ambassador, Count Alexander Benckendorff, discussed the ructions with Grey and the Prime Minister, Herbert Asquith. He reported that the politicians put protests in Britain down to propaganda disseminated by political exiles. The politicians hoped that the Reval meeting would expose the British public to more positive 'first-hand accounts' of 'Russian realities'. Whether Benckendorff shared this happy hope is not known.

For all Grey's moderation in parliament, it was the British who set stiff stipulations for the visit. Meetings would be held offshore, on the royal and imperial yachts: the *Victoria and Albert*, the *Standart* and the *Polar Star*. As Benckendorff wrote to Izvolsky: 'The British insisted on the greatest secrecy. They stipulated that the King would arrive at the Russian port on his yacht and remain on board.' In fact, he did transfer to the Russian yachts. No unauthorised craft could be closer than 1,200 feet. Only representatives of the press and three steamers carrying serenaders were allowed to move in the waters after sundown.

In a repeat of last-minute exchanges preceding the Balmoral visit, details seemed to be settled just days before. On 19th May, the British Inspector General of the Forces wrote to the Ambassador, Sir Arthur Nicolson: 'It would be of the utmost service if you could let me know the approximate dates on which the King will leave for and return from his visit to the Russian Emperor.' The meeting dates were finally confirmed as the 9th and 10th of June. Or, according to the Russian Julian calendar, (now 13 days behind) 27th and 28th of May.

In a letter headed, confusingly, with both dates – 18/31 May – Izvolsky wrote to the chargé d'affaires with the dress codes. Thankfully his subsequent schedule gave the dates solely according to the British calendar. On 9th June there would be lunch on the *Polar Star* (dress: frock coat) then dinner on the *Standart* (full dress). On 10th June, lunch would be served on the *Standart* (frock coat) and dinner on the *Victoria and Albert* (full dress).

The line-up was, for a long time, uncertain. On 26th May, Hugh O'Beirne wrote, in some dismay, to the equerry,

Sir Colonel Arthur Davidson, who had been with the imperial couple at Balmoral: 'I had counted on being able to send you the list you require by this post as I had been promised the necessary information by this evening. The promise has not been kept.'

On the 31st May, Izvolsky notified O'Beirne that the Tsar's sister, Grand Duchess Olga, and his brother, Grand Duke Michael, were due to attend. In fact the Grand Duke pulled out. Others listed included Benckendorff and the prestigious Russian Prime Minister, Pyotr Stolypin. Amongst staff from the royal household would be the imperial family's newly-appointed physician, Dr. Eugene Botkin; the head of the court chancellery, Alexander Mossolov; and Count Vladimir Fredericks, an elderly and absent-minded court minister who had served Alexander II and III.

On the 1st June, O'Beirne was ready with a further list of names: 'Herewith I send you the official list of those personages who will accompany the Tsar... at Reval... You will see certain corrections have had to be made in the list I have sent you.' He signed off, before adding: 'Since writing have been given the names of officers commanding the guard of honour by Nilov [Admiral Constantine Nilov].'

Bound up with the dizzying lists of 'personages' was the vexed issue of who should receive which medals. On the 22nd May, Davidson requested guidance from the Ambassador, Arthur Nicolson, adding: 'Anything like a wholesale distribution NEVER takes place. It would be as well therefore to obtain a rough list beforehand of those officers on whom it is suggested the King should bestow decorations.' Bertie's dislike of a wholesale distribution would contrast with the Tsar's largesse.

Meanwhile, Nicolson himself received some advice from Davidson: 'With regard to dress, you will of course bring all your uniforms and, for the yacht, blue serge suit for day time and dining jacket for evening.'

❧

Schedules and protocols had to be choreographed, as before, alongside intricate security arrangements. Rumours were emerging, once again, of planned attacks on the increasingly beleaguered Romanovs. The Russians' head of security, General Alexander Spiridovich, reported: 'The security service had heard a combat organisation [were] preparing an attack.' He added that there were other, more detailed, warnings of a group in Finland intent on murdering the Tsar.

Problems were exacerbated as the Romanovs made yet another of their last-minute travel alterations. Days before the meeting, the temperature in St Petersburg had fallen to freezing and there had been a freak snowstorm. Chary of a rough crossing, the Tsar decided that the imperial family would be better off travelling by train. Elaborate arrangements were duly put in place: half of the passengers travelling with the family were police or detectives; 7,000 Russian soldiers would line the track.

Officials, including Stolypin and Izvolsky, would be obliged to stick to the original plan, braving the sea on the cruiser *Almaz*.

In Reval itself, plans were haggled over at the Catherinental Palace, as Russian, German and Estonian officials vied for the final say. This jostling for power intensified with the

Governor of Reval making several failed attempts to bring the Russian navy under his command. All were finally agreed, however, that houses and boats should be minutely searched, and that the port would teem with detectives. Hotel managers had to report the arrival of any strangers within an hour: failure to do would result in a £3,000 fine.

No one without a permit would be allowed through the dock gates. One merchant was even forbidden from sending provisions to the *Standart*. There would be rigorous stop-and-search policies. At one point, Frederick Ponsonby was obliged to step in to protect a group of female serenaders from being strip-searched.

To add to the complexities, there was a thuggish-looking Russian called Evno Azev at the helm of the Russian security operation. When Ponsonby was asked by the British head of security who to consult, 'to ensure their majesties' safety', his reply was unhesitating: 'I told him to see the head of Russian police, Azev.'

In fact, Azev was a sort of double agent. He belonged to a revolutionary group, in which he was known as 'Frenchman' or 'Fat One'. In his memoir, the Russian head of security, Alexander Spiridovich, seems confused about Azev's role. He describes him as heading an organisation preparing an attack on the Tsar, while also alluding to 'rumours of his [Azev's] connivance with the police department'. Ponsonby later admitted: 'Afterwards he [Azev] became an agent provocator.' Azev's double life had not proven easy. On one occasion, a police handler had presented him with a jar of vodka containing the head of a suicide bomber whom he was meant to identify.

As it turned out, Azev's wheeler-dealer days were numbered. Just four months after the meeting at Reval, Prince Kropotkin and Vladimir Burtsev travelled from London to attend a 'trial', held in Paris, to determine whether or not Azev was being paid by the Tsar's secret police, the *okhrana*. On the very day of the trial, the terrorists were awaiting news of yet another plan, formulated by Azev, to assassinate the Tsar. Perhaps unsurprisingly, the plan, to be executed on the new naval cruiser *Rurik*, came to nothing.

The revolutionaries established that Azev did indeed appear on the police payroll under further aliases: 'Vinogradov', 'Kapastin', 'Philipovsky' and 'Raskin'. He was condemned, in his absence, to be hanged in a cave in Italy.

⁂

For all the British strictures, the demands of the royal yacht seemed modest. On 29th May the Commodore of the *Victoria and Albert* sent a telegram to Buckingham Palace: 'All cabins taken... counting on two police inspectors coming as usual'.

The clandestine nature of the imperial family's journey to Reval was later referred to by *The Daily Telegraph*: 'Utmost secrecy surrounded their departure – court officials and Duma leaders were unaware of the royal plans.'

It would be the first occasion, for some years, that the imperial family had been seen in public. As Spiridovich wrote: '[It was the] first major trip made by the Tsar since the uprising [Bloody Sunday]... the first time he was leaving the municipality of St Petersburg.' According to the Tsarina's lady-in-waiting, Sophie Buxhoeveden: 'The Emperor was asked by ministers not to undertake any journeys by land in the years between 1905 and 1909.'

Following Bloody Sunday, the imperial family had become ever more isolated, retreating to their palace at Tsarskoe Selo, 15 miles from St Petersburg. The massacre had provoked public outrage, and the fall in their popularity had accelerated as rumours spread of visits to the palace by the so-called 'man of God'.

Rasputin's first visit to the palace had taken place just months before the meeting at Reval. The three-year-old haemophiliac Tsarevich, Alexis, had fallen over in the Alexander Palace park and Rasputin had been summoned after doctors failed to stem the bleeding. The Tsarina's conviction that Rasputin was the only one who could save her son began with this initial apparent cure. The Tsar's sister, Olga, saw Rasputin in the children's bedroom shortly afterwards. Though she had not taken to him, she was struck by the way he prayed with the children: 'When I saw him I felt that gentleness and warmth radiated from him... It was all very impressive.'

Unfortunately, Alexis's illness was never made public and so Rasputin's role as the boy's healer was not generally known. Controversy continued to dog the 'holy man's' frequent and unexplained visits. The imperial couple tried to avoid opprobrium by meeting Rasputin at the house of the Tsarina's companion, Anna Vyrubova. Five days before the imperial family left for the meeting, the Tsar wrote in his diary: 'After dinner we went for a ride and stopped by Anya V's where we saw Grigori and spoke with him for a long time.' Alexander Mossolov, one of the courtiers at

Reval, was amongst the 'holy man's' detractors. He later made references to 'Rasputin the sinister' and railed against his table manners: 'He set to, without knife or fork.'

Tuesday 9th June 1908
The Tsar's diary: 'In the uniform of the Scots Greys I went off to visit Uncle Bertie and Aunt Alix. It was pleasant to meet them.'

The Tsar, Tsarina and their five children arrived, exhausted, at Reval station, at 7am, after travelling overnight from Peterhof. The Tsarina was described as being dressed in blue and looking more than usually out of sorts. 'We slept poorly from not being used to the railroad,' complained the Tsar in his diary. He had doubtless forgotten how 'beautifully' he had once slept on the railroad travelling south from Scotland.

The Romanovs were driven from the station to the quay, in what the Tsar referred to as a 'motorvan'. Crowds of waving children lined the streets, all the way to the imperial pavilion. There had been difficulties over the children, with the nervous governor of Reval raising a series of objections. But Spiridovich, who had been behind the scheme, had eventually triumphed. He was pleased with the result: 'It is impossible to describe the children's enthusiasm as the imperial family passed by. Their Majesties… were very touched.'

Indeed the Tsar's mother, the Dowager Empress, who

was also attending the meeting, later asked the Prime Minister, Stolypin, who it was that had organised the welcome. Spiridovich was furious to hear that the tricky Reval governor now claimed the idea as his own. A Russian admiral, who had supported Spiridovich through the arguments, was equally rattled, exclaiming: 'He's lied to the Empress, that braggart.' The Admiral added that he would no longer be providing the governor with a motorboat. 'Refuse, refuse! That will teach… [him] a lesson.'

The New York Times was full of the general excitement: 'The hill and the wooded shores of the bay were crowded with thousands and the arrival of the British King by sea and the Emperor of Russia by land was made the occasion of unbounded enthusiasm.'

The Tsar continued tranquilly: 'We immediately boarded a launch and went off to our dear *Standart*.' The 'dear *Standart*' was, at that point, the largest royal yacht in existence. It was said that every emperor, king and president in Europe had trodden, at one time or another, her polished decks. The competitive Kaiser, whose yacht was 500 tons lighter, had once hinted that the Tsar might like to hand over the *Standart*, by way of a gift. The Dowager had not been amused: 'His joke… was in very doubtful taste. I hope the Kaiser would not have the cheek to order himself a similar one here [in Denmark]. This really would be the limit – though just like him, with the tact that distinguishes him.'

The yacht was especially pristine. One of the *Standart*

officers, Nikolai Sablin, recalled that there had been a flurry of activity that morning. He described a frenzied senior boatswain, who: 'rushed around like a madman on the upper deck' issuing urgent instructions: '"Pour, well done, more, more water and scrub... better squeeze, but remember do not make any noise... all quiet, scrub... as if you do it to yourself." Then he rushed from the foredeck to the poop, with his round belly, and small quick steps where the lads seemed to be making a noise.'

Noisy cleaning had become an issue after the Tsar overheard a minister complaining about the din created by the crew in the early morning: 'When I wake up... it seems to me as if they are building a stone house of a few floors above my head, they then break it down and build it again and then break it down.' The crew were ordered to somehow curb their noise without cutting back on the rigorous 'scrub and scour'.

The imperial family had, over the years, developed a passion for their pared-down life aboard the *Standart*. The Tsar liked to sit on deck, smoking or playing dominoes; the Tsarina adored being cocooned on board with the family: 'Boysie' [the Tsar], 'my little girlies' [the four Grand Duchesses] and 'Baby love' [the Tsarevich]. On the frequent occasions when she was too poorly to sit at table, she would install herself in an armchair on the bridge. A strategically placed window enabled her to keep a watchful eye on proceedings.

The four girls formed bonds with the officers. The courtier, Mossolov, described their relations decorously: 'The young officers could better be compared with the pages or squires of dames of the middle ages.' Each of the children

Standart officer Nikolai Sablin, 'dyadya' to little Tatiana

The Tsar and Tsarina on the *Standart*

was allotted an officer, a 'dyadya' (uncle), to look after them on board. The captain was 'dyadya' to the eldest, Olga. The officer, Nikolai Sablin, who later wrote an account of his ten years on the *Standart*, was allotted Tatiana. He confessed, however, to having a particularly soft spot for Maria, who, as he reported: 'liked to sit a little, have a read and eat sweet biscuits'.

The Tsar's aide-de-camp, Count Grabbe, was in no doubt about the imperial children's enjoyment of their yachting holidays: 'To be at sea with their father – that was what constituted their greatest happiness.'

※

On their way to Reval, the King and Queen and their daughter, Victoria, endured an exceptionally challenging time at sea. Queen Alexandra and Victoria didn't seem to have much luck with their voyages; they were the ones who had suffered such a rough crossing on the *Osborne*, on their way to Balmoral in 1896.

Admiral Sir John (Jackie) Fisher gave a dramatic description of the *Victoria and Albert*'s travails in a letter to his wife, Kitty: 'We had a horrible knocking about in the North Sea. The Queen lay on deck like a corpse. Princess Victoria beckoned me to her and said she had been continuously sick and could not keep down a biscuit… everything in my cabin went mad. The armchair went head over heels through the door.'

At one point, during a lavish tea, the Queen had been thrown across the room. As Hardinge wrote: 'Suddenly there was a tremendous wave and, to my horror, I saw the

Queen thrown backwards violently on her back… followed by the tea urn, teapot, etc, all on her lap…. it was a most unpleasant incident.' Ponsonby added: 'She was thrown, chair and all into the corner… Here was a real mess, teacake, biscuits, bread and butter, sugar, etc, all collected in a heap.' He was impressed by the Queen's sangfroid: 'I persuaded her to have tea brought to her elsewhere – she retired laughing as if it was a good joke.'

After contending with sea swells, the *Victoria and Albert* was beset by fog in the Kiel canal. Ponsonby recalled: 'Cruisers and torpedo destroyers told to keep as far away as possible from the yacht'. The *Victoria and Albert* was, at this point, being preceded ceremoniously by torpedo boats and followed by HMS *Minotaur*, HMS *Achilles* and four British destroyers.

In Harold Nicolson's biography of his father Arthur, the then Ambassador in Russia, he gives an account of the Reval meeting, using 'private and semi-official correspondence'. The ascerbic Ambassador maintained a detached view of proceedings. He was unimpressed, at this point, by the acrobatics of the German torpedo boats. While the British naval officers watched in admiration, Nicolson described how the boats aimlessly 'twisted and turned'.

Detachments of German cavalry trotted alongside the *Victoria and Albert*, on the canal banks. The Danish-born Queen Alexandra, known for her anti-German sentiments, made a point of retiring to her cabins. Ponsonby described the progress of the yacht which: 'seemed to be hardly moving but cavalry [was] trotting to keep up…. [Queen] Alix stayed downstairs.' Hardinge made a sardonic but, it turned out, accurate comment about alterations then being made to the canal: 'The Germans were widening the canal so two warships could pass each other. Work would be complete in five years, so no war from Germans before 1913.'

Shortly before their arrival at Reval, Bertie summoned Arthur Nicolson to his cabin. The King took a pride in making himself comfortable at sea, giving audiences in a chintz armchair, surrounded by family photographs in silver frames. The scent of a pot of *Liliam speciosum* vied with the smell of expensive cigars.

A pressing problem had emerged: Bertie's Russian uniform was too small. The King may have felt constrained at Leith in 1896, but he was now in urgent need of a tailor. He traditionally ate too much. It was said that, after a dinner of many courses, he would retire with a cold chicken next to his bed. By the early 1900s he had a 48-inch waist and his nickname was 'Tum Tum'.

The Russian head of security, Spiridovich, gave a disparaging description of the King's subsequent difficulties: 'The tailor from the *Standart* did what he could to rectify the problem, but was only partly successful, meaning the King, strapped up in his tunic, which was visibly too tight for him and wearing the little dragoon's cap, appeared far from imposing.'

The officer, Nikolai Sablin, also reported shortcomings in the King's dress: 'His shoulder loops [were] under the epaulette straps and instead of wearing high boots he had patent leather boots with laces and patent leather gaiters. They didn't match the Russian uniform but they looked comfortable.'

No wonder the King now grilled the Ambassador on what efforts the Tsar would be making. As Nicolson put it:

Bertie, nicknamed 'TumTum', who by the
early 1900s had a 48-inch waist

Dowager Empress Marie, Edward VII and Alexandra

'Whether the Emperor would wear the uniform of the Scots Greys or whether he would appear as a Russian admiral; what decorations he would wear and in what order.' The Tsar was, of course, already wearing his controversial Scots Greys uniform.

The King questioned Nicolson closely on various aspects of Russian culture: the leading writers, musicians and scientists. He asked about Russia's progress on railways and, most importantly, its politics: what exactly were the present relations between the government and the Duma? Was the Duma a thing one should mention? Or not? He also wanted information about the Prime Minister, Stolypin, asking whether M. Stolypin spoke 'French or German or even English'.

Benckendorff had already noted that the King was eager to meet Stolypin, convinced that the meeting would create a good impression in London. Stolypin, it transpired, was equally eager, insisting: 'A rapprochement with GB is desirable, not only in the sphere of conventions but also in the domain of trade.'

The distributing of medals was an ongoing issue. Would the elderly Count Fredericks, for example, be content with a KCVO? The King's eye was, at this point, drawn 'with angered insistence' to Nicolson's Nova Scotia baronetcy badge. 'What is that bauble?' he snapped, adding, 'Never wear that bauble again.' The imperturbable Ambassador apparently wore it ever after.

The Tsar recorded his first sighting of the royal yacht

without much fanfare: 'Before 10am we saw the English detachment, coming near us from the sea, accompanied by a division of Essen's destroyers.' Ponsonby was equally blasé: 'The *V and A* arrived to find two Russian yachts and a small fleet anchored.' Nicolson reported slightly more picturesquely that the *Victoria and Albert* was 'anchored in the small but tense roadstead of Reval'. He added that English and Russian flags flew and there was an 'unsettling thunder of artillery'.

The sun shone, however, and the Russians trumpeted what they referred to as: 'Tsar's weather'. The *Standart* officer, Sablin, usually rather downbeat, was full of excitement: 'Fresh breeze tempered the heat, the weather favourable for the parade and firing of naval guns'. The *Victoria and Albert* dropped anchor between the *Standart* and the *Polar Star*. Sablin watched the British yacht's manoeuvrings in awe: 'With great skill, the *Victoria and Albert* stopped at the buoy, dropping anchor right at the spot and sinking a weathervane. At the same time [the yacht] lowered all its boats, and flags were raised very fast and flawlessly – the English captain did very well... The English vessels were painted light blue and looked very impressive.'

Despite all the preceding correspondence, as Ponsonby revealed, plans were being altered up to the last minute. Protocol, for instance, dictated that the King should greet the Russians on board the *Standart*. However, the Tsar was keen to pip his British relations to the post, arriving at the *Victoria and Albert* at 11.30 sharp. The King's talks with Nicolson were cut short. As Nicolson wrote: 'A man came to say imperial barge approaching.'

Ponsonby was put out: 'King said the ladder and steam

launch were to be got ready as soon as we anchored – but we had no chance as Tsar's boat already put off and alongside before we could lower the ladder.' He admitted that the break with protocol ended happily, as the Tsar came on board and: 'greeted his uncle and aunt most affectionately'. Nicolson noted that the band played both national anthems, and the Anglo-Russian alliance appeared to flourish: 'Everybody kissed everybody else.'

Nikolai Sablin was one of the officers who had transported the Tsar to the *Victoria and Albert*. By this time, Sablin, aged 27, had been on the *Standart* for two years. Photographs exist of him on deck and in rowing boats, smiling broadly. But a chequered military career had left him prone to moods, with a tendency to be overly critical.

As the launch drew up close to the *Victoria and Albert*, he seemed to lose his earlier enthusiasm: 'It was my first time on the English yacht, as I was replacing the flag officer who was still sick. Unfortunately, I saw nothing beyond the ladder but what I saw was enough for me to see how different it was from our boat and the others.

'The *Victoria and Albert* is a floating palace. On the upper deck you won't see a sailor or an officer. The soft furniture and flowers were throughout and in the middle of the ship, around the funnels. There was an area used by the family but the stern was used for everyday needs such as the royal kitchen, rooms for the entourage and so on. Carpets throughout and specially arranged corners, there were also little cabins, like the ones on the beaches, all expensive and first grade. Everything looked nautical and tasteful. In contrast to the *Standart*, the *Victoria and Albert* was certainly not a military ship; it was a yacht, an excellent boat designed for sailing with comfort and convenience.'

Sablin may not have been aware of the contribution of such comforts to the King's undoubted success as a diplomat. Bertie proved to be on particularly good form at Reval, not least in the way he addressed Stolypin on all the topics he had previously discussed with Nicolson. The Russian minister was duly impressed, proclaiming: '*On voit bien que c'est un homme d'état.*' He later told Hardinge that he could see why the King was 'regarded as the first statesman in Europe'. The exacting Nicolson insisted on qualifying the compliment: 'King Edward, though too superficial to be a statesman, was a supreme diplomatist.'

The head of the Russian chancellery, Alexander Mossolov, was very taken with the King's relaxed approach, giving a particular nod to Bertie's insistence on visitors being allowed to sit: 'Our Princes were accustomed, from their earliest childhood, to standing for hours and hours; after meals they formed a "circle" dead-tired.'

⁂

The British royal party now returned to the *Standart*. With all the morning's scrubbing and scouring, Spiridovich recalled a prevailing unease: 'We were very anxious about the manner in which we had to receive the English.... There was also agitation amongst our sailors, who objected to being subservient to their guests, the English sailors.'

The King's greetings to the Russian crew went slightly awry. Sablin couldn't understand much English and wouldn't have known what the King was meant to say. But he managed to spot a few glitches.

Ponsonby reported that the King, 'who knew the custom', successfully managed to greet the guard of honour with 'Good morning, children' in Russian. But, according to Sablin, the wilful Bertie then couldn't resist going off script. As he reported: 'The King and the Tsar approached aligned tall guards. Suddenly, the King stopped near an 8-vershok Peter the Great, standing at the right flank and said aloud "What a fine man." The guards, all as one, said: "Good morning, Your Royal Highness". The solemn sounds of the English anthem drowned out his answer and the King went on along the front of the crew.'

Sablin insisted he was among several crew members put out by Bertie's lofty attitude: 'The Russian hosts were treated most graciously and in a friendly manner. But it was felt that Edward showed some condescension towards his nephew – he seemed to be patronising him.' He insisted, further, that the King was too intimate with the rest of the family: 'But he was on familiar terms with the Empress, as if she were ONE OF THEM... he warmly hugged and kissed the Empress and then took a closer look at our Princesses, who looked a bit embarrassed. Then he walked over to the heir, took him in his arms and kissed him.'

In fact, Sablin's critical descriptions of the King's manner are not borne out by any of the other accounts. The general view was that the two monarchs seemed to get along very well. Nicolson reported wryly that the King managed to make the Tsar feel every bit the 'highly successful nephew'. This he achieved, according to Nicolson, simply by steering clear of the 'political conversations' the Tsar so dreaded: 'The mere fact that he [Bertie] avoided all

Bertie and the Tsar on deck

The King reportedly managed to make the Tsar feel
every bit the 'highly successful nephew'

political questions inspired the timid little autocrat with confidence, gratitude and relief.'

There had been arguments, before the meeting, about whether the Tsar should be challenged on the controversial issue of Jewish pogroms. On 3rd June, Lord Rothschild and his two brothers, Alfred and Leopold, wrote to the King complaining about the plight of Jews in Russia. They pleaded with the King to raise the issue with the Tsar.

Knollys had replied immediately: 'The King desires me to let you know, in reply to the letter which you, Alfred and Leo have written to him, that he will speak to Sir Charles Hardinge and Sir Arthur Nicolson respecting the question which you have brought before him. The subject would be a very delicate one for him to bring before the Emperor of Russia, and it is, moreover, one of considerable political importance. His Majesty feels, therefore, that it would not be constitutionally correct or proper for him to speak to the Emperor or to his advisers on the matter unless he did so with the full concurrence of Sir C. Hardinge and Sir Arthur Nicolson, both of whom accompany him to Reval.'

In the end, the King and Nicolson both managed to raise the matter with Stolypin. To the Rothschilds' disappointment, however, Stolypin's replies never went beyond vague assurances. British politicians were divided in their view as to whether the matter should have been raised at all. Some felt the King had overstepped the mark, others that he had shown moral courage.

Further controversy surrounded another of the King's

Jewish friends, Ernest Cassel. The pair had dined together the night before Bertie left for Reval and Cassel had expressed an interest in a Russian loan. Hardinge was among those who expressed worry that the King might pull strings on Cassell's behalf. But, as it turned out, the King did no more than ask the Tsar to receive his friend if he visited St Petersburg. What the Tsar felt about the request, after taking issue with Bertie's 'queer guests' at Sandringham, is not known. When the prickly Kaiser heard about the shenanigans, however, he described his Uncle Bertie as 'a jobber in stocks and shares' who counted on making personal profit out of a Russian loan.

The King, at this point, generally seemed to prefer to stick to pleasantries. Members of the Russian party were struck by how much more relaxed the Tsar seemed with the King than he was with the Kaiser. As Hardinge reported: 'Several of the Tsar's suite, personal friends, commented to me upon the marked difference in the Emperor's spirits and attitudes during the King's visit to Reval compared with what they were at the Emperor's recent visit to the German Emperor at Swinmunde, where he felt anxiety all the time as to what might be unexpectedly sprung upon him.'

Mossolov felt that the English court compared favourably to the German court: 'Except when on duty, no account was taken of rank. What a contrast there was between the visits of Wilhelm II and the reception of the King and Queen at Reval.'

Sablin was, as ever, in disagreement. He found Bertie less

polished than either the German Kaiser or the French president. In his view, the monarchs greeted each other stiffly: 'Edward shook hands with the Emperor but they didn't embrace, as had happened with Wilhelm… The Kaiser did his greetings in Russian very well. The French president spoke a greeting in French and the people could catch the end of the phrase and answer gracefully.' Sablin admitted that the King showed a passing interest in the Russian ships: the cruiser *Admiral Makarov* and ice breaker *Ermak*. But, he added: '… he did not speak as authoritatively as the Kaiser.'

The King had always had his own reservations about the Kaiser. During sensitive discussions as to where his meeting with the Tsar should take place, Bertie had made it clear that he was determined to keep the Kaiser at bay. As Benckendorff reported: 'The King said [the meeting] had to be sufficiently far from the German border to avoid the Kaiser descending on the two monarchs.'

❧

Arthur Nicolson had, by this time, been Ambassador in St Petersburg for two years. He was nearly 60 and slightly stooped, noticeably smaller than his fellow diplomats and courtiers. His lack of height did not diminish his authority. He expressed himself loftily, making full use of a battery of waspish comments. His initial impression was that the imperial couple were on relatively good form, but he couldn't resist adding unflattering references to the Tsarina: 'The Emperor was gay and at his ease. Even the Empress, a shy and sulky woman, inclined to unbend. She walked across that carpeted deck with that stooping movement adopted by affectionate women who are much taller than their husbands; the whites of her eyes yellow with prolonged dyspepsia; she pointed at things and people with a lace sunshade.'

He proved almost uniquely unsusceptible to the charms of the beautiful imperial children: 'The Tsarevich went off and played with Derevenko, the sailor friend who never left him,' he reported flatly. 'The Grand Duchesses, in English schoolgirl clothes, simpered like English schoolgirls.'

This Englishness of the young Grand Duchesses, who had never been to England, might have been down to the influence of their anglophile mother. The girls had also been receiving regular lessons from an English tutor, John Epps, for four years. Mr Epps struggled to keep charge, particularly when the girls argued over who was to be allowed to use his exotic pen. As he recalled fondly: 'A great deal of tact was necessary to maintain order.' During one session, he taught them how English words might be combined, as in spoon-ful. When he asked them if they now understood combinations, he was rather thrown by their cheeky response: 'Oh yes, we wear them.'

The Tsar's doughty mother, the 60-year-old Dowager Empress, arrived at Reval an hour after the Tsar, travelling by train with her daughter, the Tsar's sister, Olga. Mossolov recalled how much the Dowager looked forward to seeing her sister, Queen Alexandra, and her niece, Princess Victoria. Sablin confirmed: 'They were very amicable towards each other and the daughter [Princess] Victoria, was very much loved by both our empresses.'

Sablin watched the interaction between the Dowager

and the Tsarina and the 'English ladies', and registered the Dowager's attempts to keep a low profile: '[The Dowager] tried to stay on the sidelines because Alexandra Feoderovna [the Tsarina] was meant to be the hostess and the English ladies also treated her respectfully to reflect her position.' There had always been an element of rivalry between the Dowager and the Tsarina. One of their first arguments had been over protocol, with the Dowager refusing to hand over some jewels. There followed a dispute over whose name should come immediately after the Tsar's during prayers.

Sablin noted the contrasts in the women's dress: 'The English ladies were dressed very modestly, you could even say old-fashioned.' The Dowager may have agreed that the women were dressed modestly, but she would not have considered their clothing old-fashioned. She was a fan of

OTMA with their aunt Olga and grandmother

The Tsarina with female entourage on the *Standart*

The Grand Duchesses with Princess Victoria

British fashion, refusing to go anywhere but London for her toque hats and wigs.

Indeed the Dowager was, at this point, flush with a rekindled passion for Britain. She had enjoyed British holidays after her sister's marriage to Bertie, but then had been forced, for political reasons, to stay away. In March 1907, she had enjoyed a three-week stay with her sister, writing rapturously to Nicky: 'We went by car... I have no words to describe how magnificent it all is. Aunt Alix's rooms are remarkably beautiful and cosy. I must say they are the same here, at Buckingham Palace. Everything is so tastefully and artistically arranged, it makes one's mouth water to see all this magnificence.

'I do wish you too could come over here for a little, to breathe another air. How good that would be! I myself feel as if I were a different person – and 20 years younger!'

Her daughter Olga, was not particularly anglophile, but she had a strong British influence in her life: her nanny, 'Nana', Elizabeth Francklin, the daughter of an innkeeper in Bedfordshire. Recommended by her aunt, Alexandra, she had tended Olga from birth.

The Dowager, during her days as tsarina, had, at one point, tried to dispatch Nana, believing that she and her charge were too attached. She had insisted that, as Olga was well into her teens, she must be attended by a lady-in-waiting. But Olga had proven obdurate, shouting at her mother: 'Alicky had her Mrs Orchard brought to Russia. What shall I do without Nana? If you send her away I will run away myself. I will elope with a palace sweep. I will go and peel potatoes in someone's kitchen or offer myself as a kennel maid to one of the society ladies in St Petersburg.

And I am sure Nicky will be on my side.'

Olga won her battle and, in her late 20s, was still obeying Mrs Francklin's rules on coughs and colds: 'Nana says I mustn't go out.' The Dowager never quite recovered from her worsting, referring to the beleaguered nanny as 'that odious woman'.

Nana introduced English teas to the imperial nursery: bread before cake was apparently the strictest rule. She ordered golden syrup from England and, at Christmas, insisted on making a plum pudding.

While enjoying the teas and puddings, Olga evidently found some of Nana's English attitudes less appealing. At Peterhof, the pair would occasionally come upon soldiers bathing and washing their clothes in the rivers: 'Caught by surprise, the men would scramble out of the water, not to get their clothes, but to grab their caps, which they would jam on their wet heads. Then, smartly standing at attention, they would salute and shout... Only Nana, with her proper British ways, thought the sight "revolting" and looked away,' she recalled.

Nana and Orchie became the best of friends, discussing 'their' children over cups of tea. Perhaps it was as well that the outspoken Margaret Eager was not included in the nannies' tea parties. She would undoubtedly have been bored by the conversation and irritated by the elderly Orchie, who she subsequently described in a cold note to a Russian friend: 'Mrs Orchard is here – she forgets so much and her nose is so purple, I'm afraid it's the heart that causes that.'

Grand Duchess Olga didn't share Nana's fondness for Orchie either: 'She [Miss Orchard] was most dictatorial and in the end left the palace in a huff. There followed spells of complete chaos.'

At the time of the Reval meeting, Olga was a youthful 26, locked in a loveless marriage with the homosexual Grand Duke Peter of Oldenburg. It would have come as no surprise therefore that she was ready to make the most of a new friendship, during the trip, with the glamorous English Admiral, Sir John Fisher.

The Admiral, known as 'Jackie' Fisher, was much older than her, at 57, but still handsome and a keen dancer. She had met him, some months before, in Karlsbad, in Germany, succumbing to his charms as he passed on dancing tips. She confessed later: 'I particularly enjoyed meeting Admiral Fisher again.' The feelings were evidently mutual. A week before the Reval meeting, Fisher wrote excitedly to a Mrs Spender: 'The King has sweetly asked me to go to Russia with him, which is lovely, as the Queen has telegraphed for that Grand Duchess I am in love with to come and meet me.'

⚜

Lunch was served on the Dowager's yacht, the *Polar Star*. As the Tsar reported briefly: 'After mutual presentations of our suites and conversation, we broke up, changed into frock coats and met for lunch on the *Polar Star*.' It is not clear whether Bertie, at this point, also took the opportunity to remove his constraining Russian uniform.

Prince Felix Yusupov, later famous for murdering Rasputin, gives a vivid description of the King's discomfort at table that day. Yusupov was not actually at Reval, so he must have heard details through his friends at court. His description gives every indication that the King was, indeed, still stuffed into his Russian uniform. He claimed the King dined: 'in a state of semi-suffocation and in a very bad temper'.

Ponsonby was not taken with the *Polar Star*. While Sablin had found the *Victoria and Albert* too fancy, Ponsonby decreed the *Polar Star* too military. The yacht, he wrote, was: 'most beautifully fitted up but elaborate military arrangements on board'.

The lunch menu was headed, confusingly, 'Dejeuner du 27 Mai 1908'. Despite all the spirit of accord, the Russian hosts were only noting their own date. The menus were in occasionally idiosyncratic French. The food sounded exotic: 'Potages: Princesse, Consommé à la Toulouse, Petits patés. Homard au Champagne, froid. Roulettes de Gélinotte Truffées en Vol-au-vent, Canards Nantais aux Petits Pois. Pêches à la Vanille at Purée de Fraises Glacée. Fromages. Dessert'. Ponsonby, however, mentioned only caviar sandwiches and an unappetising drink: 'kirsch which tasted of boot varnish'.

Following his disappointing lunch, Ponsonby returned to the *Victoria and Albert* to meet the head of the British police, Patrick Quinn. He suggested, perhaps unwisely, that Quinn contact the slippery Azev. The police, he wrote: 'recommended [that an] officer [be] posted on every gangway on the yacht to see who came on board – uniform no criterion. Every individual should be scrutinised and passed.' He was irritated to discover that he would not be allowed to go ashore: 'tiresome, as I should very much like to have seen the town of Reval which looked most picturesque.'

Sablin insisted that tea, or the 'Five o'clock', as he called it, was served on the *Standart* at, naturally, 5pm. The Tsar's 'Five o'clock' traditionally comprised one glass of tea with milk and one without. It is hard to know why Sablin, who had never been to England, felt he was such an authority on British customs. But he stood firm on tea-time: 'It was quite informal, because it is the most favourite and traditional English pastime, one cannot imagine English life without the "Five o'clocks".'

The Tsar revealed that tea was, in fact, served on the 'English yacht'. It is possible that Sablin had a memory lapse; on the other hand, he might simply have been unable to resist a discourse on 'Five o'clocks' and an accompanying dig at English pastimes.

Whatever the case, the Tsar was upset that he had to go to the *Victoria and Albert* alone, as his wife was suffering, once again, from sciatica: 'Alix unfortunately was not able to come due to the pains in her legs.' Despite Nicolson's earlier claim that the Tsarina was 'inclined to unbend', there were several reports that she was 'fatigued by her journey' to Reval. Sablin had seen the Empress that morning, for the first time in several months, and was not impressed: 'We already noticed that the Empress didn't feel that great.'

The Tsarina's recurring ailments put the whole of her family under a strain. But she stuck to her curiously positive view, writing of the benefits of sick mothers to her daughter, Maria: 'I know it's dull having an invalid mother, but it teaches you all to be loving and gentle.' Her devoted daughters were not satisfied. They all worried about her heart, which she would grimly register, on a scale of one to three. And they missed her company. As Olga complained in a note: 'So sorry that never see you alone, Mama dear... what is to be done if there is not time, and neither can I hear the dear words which sweet Mama could tell me.' Tatiana also wrote, displaying some patchy English: 'I hope you wont be today very tied and that you can get up to dinner.... I am always so awfuy sorry when you are tied and when you can't get up [sic].'

The Tsarina's malaise was exacerbated by the all too justifiable anxiety she felt for her son. Minor cuts or bruises could have dangerous consequences for the haemophiliac Alexis.

The British royals returned to the *Standart* for dinner, as the Tsar recorded baldly: 'At 8.30 there was a dinner on our ship with toasts.'

Sablin began his evening in unusually good heart: 'At exactly 8pm the magnificent English motorboat again delivered the royal relatives to the *Standart*.' He was captivated by the foreman of the English boat: 'an old man, covered with medals with a huge belly and the typical face of an English sea dog. He always stood at the steering wheel of the King's motorboat and, apparently, Edward VII was very fond of him. It was felt there was a special relationship between them as between old serving servants and a good gentleman.'

He was won over by the British party, even succumbing to the King: 'Contrary to normal British stiffness, the dinner was very lively. The King for that matter was charmingly sweet.' It was probably at this juncture that Sablin began making the odd skittish reference to 'Uncle Eddie'.

The dinner menu was headed, as on the *Polar Star*, solely with the Russian date: 'Diner du 27 Mai 1908'; on some, 9th June was written in pencil alongside. The menu was, once again, impressive: 'Potages: Pierre le Grand Marie Louise, Petites Patés, Sterlet de la Doina au Champagne, Selle de Chevreuil Grand Veneur, Parfait de Foie gras au Porto, Punch au Thé Vert, Roti-Poulardes du Mans et Becasses, Salade, Asperges d'Argenteuil Sauce Mousseline, Pêches à la Coque, Glaces à la Parisienne, Desserts.'

Sablin was especially taken with the King's 'subtle humour': 'When wild goat with sweet blackcurrant jelly was served with the amazing Cumberland sauce, the famous gastronomist [the King] said: "You could eat your own mother with this sauce." Pierre Kyba, the Maitre d', was very pleased.' Nicolson, however, perhaps predictably, disliked all the dishes. He would presumably have found the Cumberland sauce even less enticing served with (or over) Queen Victoria. As he reported bleakly: 'Banquet that evening on the *Standart*. The food was bad.'

The programme of music to be played, presumably by the *Standart* orchestra, was listed mostly, stylishly, in French and featured the peasants' chorus from Borodin's Prince Igor: '1. Wagner: ouverture de l'op *La Vaisseau Fantome*. 2. Borodine: La Choeur de Paysans de l'op *Prince Igor*. 3. Glazounov: divertissements du ballet *Raymonde*. 4. Grieg: Anitras Dans and Dovregubbens Hall from *Peer Gynt*. 5. Liszt: 2-me Rhapsodie hongroise. 6. Gounod: Entr'acte at Danse de Bacchantes de l'op *Philemon et Baucis*.'

Speeches followed, with the Tsar reading from a painstakingly prepared script and the King delivering his off the cuff. Copies of the Tsar's speech were distributed to journalists but there was no equivalent record, obviously, for the King. When Admiral Fisher asked Bertie why he had no aide-memoir, the King replied that he had once memorised a speech for the French president, to be delivered in the garden of Buckingham Palace. When he rose to speak, he found, to his horror, that he had forgotten every word. He recalled that he: '… had to keep on beginning again at the beginning… Never again'.

The Tsar's speech was predictable: 'It is with feelings of the deepest satisfaction and pleasure that I welcome Your Majesty and Her Majesty the Queen to Russian waters. I trust that this meeting, while strengthening the many and strong ties which unite our houses, will have the happy results of drawing our countries closer together, and of promoting and maintaining the peace of the world.

'In the course of the past year several questions of equal moment both to Russia and to England have been satisfactorily settled by our governments. I am certain that Your Majesty appreciates as highly as I do the value of the agreements, for, notwithstanding their limited scope, they cannot but help to spread among our two countries feelings of mutual goodwill and confidence. I drink to the health of Your Majesty and of the Queen and to the prosperity of the royal family and of the British nation.'

The King's speech, noted down by Ponsonby, was warmer in tone: 'I thank Your Majesty most heartily on behalf of the Queen and myself for the cordial manner in which you have welcomed us in the waters of the Baltic and for the affectionate words in which you have proposed our healths. I have the happiest recollections of the welcome which I received on the occasions of my previous visit to Russia at the hands of your illustrious grandfather, your beloved father, and yourself, and it is a source of the sincerest gratification to me to have this opportunity of meeting your majesties again.

'I most heartily endorse every word that fell from Your Majesty's lips with regard to the [Anglo-Russian] convention recently concluded between our two governments. I believe it will serve to knit more closely the bonds that unite the people of our two countries, and I am certain that it will conduce to the satisfactory settlement in an amicable manner of some momentous questions in the future. I am convinced that it will not only tend to draw our two countries more closely together but will help very greatly towards the maintenance of the general peace of the world.

'I hope this meeting may be followed before long by another opportunity of meeting your majesties. I drink to the health of your majesties; to that of the Empress Marie Feodorovna, and the members of the imperial family and, above, all to the welfare and prosperity of your great empire.'

It was at this point that Sablin's view of 'Uncle Eddie' took the inevitable downturn. He cannot have understood much of either of the speeches, which were both delivered in English. He was adamant, nonetheless, that the King was outshone by the Tsar: 'The Emperor's answer was very short and from his expression could be seen that he thought about the seriousness and importance of the events that were planned for the future, but he spoke openheartedly.'

The King's extemporising, on the other hand, he deemed disrespectful, insisting, as usual, that his negative view was generally shared. Sablin was sure that the King held notes which he, perversely, refused to use: 'Edward VII spoke softly and lazily. It was felt he didn't attach importance to the fact that he was forced to stick to the minister's speech, which he held in his hand.' Needless to say, Ponsonby disagreed with Sablin: 'King made impressive speech... proposing the health of the Emperor.'

Among the party there was also Olga, Queen of Greece, whose son, Andrew, had married the Tsarina's lively niece, Alice, five years previously. Their son Philip, born 13 years later, would be the future Duke of Edinburgh. The Queen of Greece came armed with celebratory photographs of herself to give to the crew, signed 'Olga, Reval 1908'.

The diners repaired to the deck, where they could enjoy the illumination of the ships. As *The New York Times*

Olga, Queen of Greece, who came armed with this
photograph of herself to give to the crew

reported: 'Warships were brilliantly illuminated and the yachts *Polar Star* and *Alexandra* displayed special electrical effects'. Sablin hoped they would appreciate the *Standart's* intricate water feature: 'After dinner, coffee and cigars on quarterdeck. Talking quietly, sitting among the greenery, flowers and gurgling of a small cascade – the pride of our mechanics.'

Sadly the sound of quiet talking and gurgling was soon drowned out by some serenaders. As Ponsonby recalled: 'After dinner the two monarchs stood on deck while a steamer full of some choral society came and sang weird Russian songs.'

Ponsonby had earlier discussed this same choral society with the head of the British police, Quinn, and been told that the Russian police intended to have all the members strip-searched: 'When Mr Quinn came and told me this, I felt there might be a row in England and questions might be asked in the house about it. The greater part of the singers were ladies and I wondered what would be said if, when the Russian Emperor came to England, and some choral society asked leave to serenade him, our police insisted on stripping them and searching them… Mr Quinn said Russian police had agreed to give up this stringent measure.'

Needless to say, Sablin found the serenading worse than weird: 'Under *Standart's* stern, yard ships sailing with the brightly dressed public and the local choral society – various Schwarzkopfs – played horrible music. The entire Reval roadstead was filled with lights coming from all the vessels with the music played in honour of the foreign guests.' Sablin never revealed which aspect of the music he found 'horrible', but it can't have been its foreignness: the

Reval musical society programme boasts balalaika accompaniments and an opening song entitled: 'Let the Tsar live forever'.

Nicolson was convinced that the King found the music tedious: 'They were serenaded afterwards by certain carefully chosen inhabitants of Reval who appeared in a tug. King Edward, who only cared for Puccini, was bored. He fiddled in an abstract manner with the gold bracelet on his left wrist.'

The New York Times seems to have been alone in its appreciation. 'Boatloads of German, Estonian and Russian residents steamed out in the roadstead and serenaded the royal visitors with national folk songs and village roundelays, the singing of the Estonians being particularly pleasing as the melody floated over the moonlit waters.'

The Tsarina's attitude to the serenaders is not known, but it was at this point in the evening that she surrendered to a loud fit of tears. Hardinge heard the sound of weeping as he took a solitary walk around the deck. As the former Ambassador to Russia, from 1904 to 1906, he would have been relatively familiar with her moods; he was also 14 years her senior. Both elements would have played a part in his bold decision to approach her. As he recalled: 'The Empress was in a state of nervous hysteria for, at a dance after dinner on board the *Standart*, when I happened to wander around the other side of the deck, I heard sobs and found the Empress sitting alone and weeping, and on my offer to obtain help she asked to be left alone.'

Towards the end of the evening, the 'highly successful nephew' appeared to suffer a setback, when he tried and failed to attract his uncle's attention. Sablin was infuriated as he watched the King talking, instead, to a random member of the *Standart* crew: 'Ministers and other officials gathered around the Tsar expecting to be summoned to the anticipated informal meeting of the monarchs… The King lit a large cigar, took a seat in one of the chairs near the royal cabins. Suddenly he stood up and slowly walked towards the watchman. Standing to the right of the ladder, Edward VII began animatedly talking to the astonished sailor about something, puffing a fragrant cigar from time to time. Everyone was watching the scene with amazement.

'The Tsar tried to approach His Majesty several times but the King pretended not to notice and became even more engaged in conversation. The ministers concluded that no conference would be held – neither today nor in the future – and the King decided without them what was required for the good of England. The King entertained the simple Russian sailor with his conversation for a quarter of an hour.'

When the party left the *Standart*, Bertie made a point of taking leave of his new acquaintance. 'The King quickly turned away and went to say goodbye to the Empress, gave a friendly hug to the Emperor and went to the ladder. A few words, with a sweet smile, short bows to the retinue and the minister, then the King, when passing the watchman, said: "Goodbye, goodbye dear fellow". Turning once again, Edward VII patted his astonished companion on the back and gave him a half smoked fragrant cigar and then skipped into his motorboat.'

Sablin added a bizarre detail: 'As the motorboat pulled away, a hand came out of a lower porthole and handed the coxswain a ginger kitten. As he recounted: "'Uncle Eddie" pressed it to his chest.'

After the King left, the captain of the *Standart*, also, coincidentally, called Nikolai Sablin, immediately quizzed the privileged sailor: 'The captain approached the watchman, "What was the King saying to you?". "I do not know," replied the King's famous companion, in his own language, beaming broadly. "Good for you brother…" said the usually stern captain and awarded the lucky man a brand new rouble.'

❦

The Tsar gave an unusually cheerful account of his day. He did not seem to have noticed any slights from his uncle and was probably unaware of his wife's fit of tears: 'The day remained marvellous, in a dead like stillness. The impression of the day was the very best.' Ponsonby was captivated by the white night: 'rather weird being broad daylight – sun does not set till 11.30 at night. There was a beautiful, red sky.' Sablin added a final, vivid picture: 'The white night lit up the roadstead, and the bulky figure of Edward VII paced rhythmically on the upper promenade deck of *V and A*.'

Wednesday 10th June
The Tsar's diary: 'A divine day again'.

At 11.30am the Tsar and Tsarina were obliged to receive delegations from Reval. The head of security, Spiridovich, noted the Tsarina's malaise. Was it her legs again? Or her upset from the night before? Spiridovich wrote: 'Accompanied by the Empress, the Emperor inspected the circle formed by the delegates, exchanging a few words with each of them. After him, the Empress had little to add, she spoke very little, every so often she would smile, but it seems a forced smile. She was visibly uncomfortable and ill at ease, those seeing her for the first time could have mistaken this for arrogance. "She was a sorry sight," one of the delegates who adored the Emperor and his family told me later.'

To add to her discomfort, the Tsarina was the victim of a social gaffe. As Spiridovich added: 'The peasant representatives included one of His Majesty's former Uhlans. The Emperor, who had an astonishing memory, recognised him, and told the Empress, in English, to extend her hand to the Uhlan. The Empress did so, and the Uhlan just shook it, without kissing it. Everyone felt embarrassed but no one knew how to signal to the Uhlan to draw his attention to the lack of protocol he had just made.'

The British party returned to the *Standart* for what the Tsar referred to prosaically as 'a big lunch' at 1pm. 'Dejeuner du 28 Mai 1908' comprised: 'Potage Crème Printanière, Petits Patés, Truite Taymine Italienne Sce Verte, Petits Poulets de Grains Clamart, Selle de Bebague Richelieu, Macedoine de Fruits au Champagne, Mousseline Victoria,

Dessert'. It was during this meal that the King hit upon the happy notion of giving the Tsar another British title. Hardinge fondly recalled receiving a note from the King asking: 'Whether I did not think he might appoint the Emperor to be a British admiral of the fleet. (This menu I treasure amongst my papers). I at once replied that I thought the idea an excellent one.' Fisher gave a colourful description of Nicky's reaction: 'Tsar like a child in his delight at having been made admiral of the fleet'. The Tsar himself, as ever, gave little away in his own diary: 'Uncle Bertie appointed me Admiral of the English navy.'

The excellent idea proved controversial. On June 10th, the Prime Minister, Herbert Asquith, wrote Knollys a stiff letter, headed 'secret'. He had heard of the appointment in a cypher telegram from Hardinge: 'As you well know this Russian visit has, from the first, been a delicate affair. We have done our best to remove apprehension and doubts, but where such grave issues are involved, I should not be doing my duty if I did not suggest, and even urge, the desirability of preliminary notice.'

Upon his return, the King was informed by Asquith directly that the appointment, 'off his own bat', had been unconstitutional. Bertie breezily instructed Knollys to write a letter of apology, explaining that he was 'totally unaware of the constitutional point'. He added that he: 'regretted that he had, without knowing it, acted irregularly'. Beckendorff gave his own account of the repercussions: 'The radicals and the British court blamed Grey, for he had sent the King on the visit without a responsible minister at his side.' The forthright Admiral Fisher, of course, had his own view: 'It's a jolly good thing we have a King who knows how to act, as cabinet ministers seem to me always like frightened rabbits.'

⚜

Nicolson left some scant details: 'Large lunch on *Standart;* Izvolsky and Hardinge discussed the Straits.' Hardinge would insist that he was: 'always prepared to discuss the Straits in an amicable spirit'. He clearly did keep the discussions amicable, even though he and Izvolsky were in basic disagreement. In an echo of the Tsar's talks with Salisbury at Balmoral, Izvolsky held the view that the Turkish Straits should be open only to Russians, while Hardinge wanted them open to all. Hardinge's description of the great Izvolsky indicates that he succeeded in gaining the upper hand: 'He [Izvolsky] struck me as very able, adroit but extremely timid… any suggestion which I made to him was at once set aside as requiring careful study.'

Hardinge broached easier topics with the Tsar: 'He was enthusiastic over the Anglo-Russia agreement [and he] foretold close cooperation in the future between the two countries.' Hardinge brought up the positive Russian press coverage preceding the visit: 'On my saying I was surprised at the support of the "bitterest foe of England" (*Novoe Vremya*), His Majesty admitted that he was also astonished at the rapidity with which the feeling had spread and that he had never been so surprised as when he had read recently in a chauvinistic "rag" called the *Sviet* a warm article in praise of England and urging closer relations between the two countries.' In fact, the *Sviet* had also been quoted by Hugh O'Beirne as referring to the 'traditional enmity of England'.

In the growing spirit of accord, the Tsar told Hardinge that he looked forward, at some stage, to meeting Edward Grey.

Hardinge commented, once again, on the Tsar's well-being: '[He] looked extraordinarily well and in the best possible spirits.' If he was struck by the contrast in mood between the Tsar and his tearful wife of the night before, he made no reference to it.

Meanwhile, Ponsonby made great strides with Stolypin, who he described as: 'a grave, splendid-looking man with a long grey beard'. Stolypin told Ponsonby of his refusal to be intimidated by the nihilists who had attacked him just two years before: the resulting explosion had cost his daughter her leg. Ponsonby was full of admiration: 'He said that if he lived in fear of his life, his life wouldn't be worth living. He asked me a good deal about English politics, seemed to be very well versed in everything going on in England.' Stolypin himself was very taken with the Queen's lady-in-waiting, 'la charmante Lady Antrim', later sending her photographs of Reval. He spoke of 'les belles journées... dont je garde un souvenir inoubliable'.

It was probably during this lunch that the beleaguered Tsarina suffered a further blow, as the King told her that the little Grand Duchesses had poor English accents. The criticism would have been especially offensive coming from Bertie, whose own speech was distinctly Germanic. The Tsar's nephew, Prince Dmitri, never forgot the King's regular exclamation: 'Ach!'

Bertie's comments, overheard by Arthur Nicolson, went

down badly. It is impossible to know the reasons for the Tsarina's extreme response. Was she in pain again? Was it her generally low mood? Did she worry that his criticism was justified? In any case, her decision was immediate and uncompromising: the English tutor, Mr Epps, must go.

Epps has since been accused of giving the two elder Grand Duchesses a 'strange Scottish twang'. But his relation, Janet Epps, doubts Epps ever set foot in Scotland. He was raised in Kent and attended a private boys' grammar school, before doing a course at a teacher training institute in London. Janet Epps is inclined to lay the blame elsewhere: 'They probably got their accent from the Irish nanny.' This could have been Miss Eager, from Limerick, or Orchie, from Dublin. Orchie had been at the court, intermittently, since little Olga's birth, in 1895, and stayed, for a short time, after Miss Eager's departure in 1904.

Epps's replacement, the Yorkshireman Sydney Gibbes, mentioned nothing of his predecessor's accent, but he was more than willing to give details of speech defects: 'Epps was a nice man but he was totally uneducated. He couldn't pronounce "g" at the end of a word and he couldn't pronounce "h" at the beginning without an enormous effort, which was prominent in all his conversation.' Gibbes further accused Epps of being given to gossip: 'He used to tell tales and I remember his coming once to see us and telling tales about the Grand Duchess Anastasia... She was a bright lively girl and everybody's favourite. It was a very unprofessional thing for him to speak of the palace to people outside.'

Before moving to the palace, Epps had taught at the Lyceum high school for Young Nobles in St Petersburg. The

Grand Duchesses may well have proved more challenging than the young nobles. When not arguing about his exotic pen, the girls would stand on the window sills then jump off, obliging Epps, then pushing 60, to catch them. 'But they were bonnie children and possessed "avoir du pois" [weight] so it was a tiring game,' he recalled.

With all his difficulties, Mr Epps had become a favourite at court. The Tsarina would have been reluctant to fire him, but she may have felt compelled to be seen to do something. Miss Eager had already been sent away and Orchie had died. Mr Epps seemed to accept his dismissal with good grace. As Janet Epps says: 'He quite understood that he had to be the scapegoat in this situation.'

Days before the meeting, the Tsarina had celebrated her 36th birthday, with the Tsar writing hopefully in his diary: 'Dear Alix's birthday. Lord grant her health, strength and fortitude.' Epps received a hand-scrawled telegram thanking him for his birthday greeting: 'Many thanks for congratulations, Alexandra.' He would leave, weeks later, with a large ruby ring for his troubles.

At some point during the meeting at Reval, there was the inevitable exchange of lavish gifts. The King presented his nephew with a sword made by Wilkinson, engraved with the words: 'For his Imperial Majesty Emperor of All Russia from His Loving Uncle Edward, Reval 1908'. Nicky, in turn, gave his uncle a nephrite vase set with cabochon moonstones and chalcedony, which had been bought on 23rd May at a cost of 2,500 roubles. Other Russian gifts included cigarette boxes and cigar boxes, bronze busts for Count Benckendorff and Charles Hardinge, and enamelled spoons for Mrs Knollys.

Spirodovich was thrilled to receive a medal, though he failed to understand most of the accompanying speech. He reported that he was taken to one of the British ships by the head of the secret service. He was then introduced to: 'an elderly Englishman who appeared honourable and important... The honourable Englishman read something small out to me in his language, of which I did not understand a single word, and after that he ceremoniously presented me with the Commander's Cross of the Order of Victoria with a certificate, letter and statutes. Once this was done, he congratulated me, this time in French, for having deserved this royal order, I thanked him, was then led back to the ladder, and returned home... I was very proud of the decoration and the circumstances in which I had received it.'

The receipt of his own medal did little to stem Sablin's niggles: 'The British are very sparing with their honours. Apart from the Captain, the only other officers who received them were the senior officer and chief of guard.' He tut-tutted over muddles with the ranking: 'I received Victorian Order Class 4, and the senior officer, more senior than me, the Victorian Order Class 5. Chagin [the naval Admiral] understood to correct this misunderstanding, which I readily agreed to.'

Sablin pointed out that, while the British were so sparing, the imperial couple were always finding new reasons to present gifts. The Tsarina was as generous as her husband: 'Starting that year – 1908 – before the end of the season, Their Majesties would have dinner with us in our wardroom and to show gratitude for the voyages, they would give us something – a loving cup or wine glasses or flower vases, etc.

'Similarly, to express friendship and in memory of our good relationship, the entourage presented the wardroom with souvenirs: Fabergé cigarette boxes with an image of the yachts, an album with silhouettes of everyone who was on board, which were cut out by the skilful adjutant.'

The Tsar had to be prevented from making more presentations on the British ship, the *Minotaur*, which had accompanied the *Victoria and Albert*. Admiral Fisher mentioned the visit in a letter to his friend, the Liberal politician Reginald McKenna: 'He went all over her. He wanted to decorate the whole crew, but the King restrained him.' The Tsar recorded baldly: 'I sailed on their cruiser, the *Minotaur*, and looked it over from the outside. Then I transferred to the turbine yacht, the [Russian] *Alexandra*, on which all the relatives were.'

The second 'Five o'clock' took place on the *Polar Star*. As the Tsar wrote: 'We departed to the *Polar Star* where Mama had tea set up.' The imperial family then returned to the *Standart* and the Tsar did what he enjoyed best: 'played with the children'. The *Standart* was well equipped with games: Alexis's playroom boasted a blue and red kite, battledore and shuttlecock, deck billiards and nine bunches of straws for blowing bubbles.

Communal games included bingo sessions, arranged either by the officers or the Tsar's sister Olga, perhaps anxious for distraction from her unhappy home life. There was an excuse for yet more gifts, as the Tsarina awarded prizes from her chaise longue. Sablin wrote: 'It is impossible to forget the pleasure of the bingo evenings. Everyone was calling numbers and, when someone won, the Empress would give a prize, a little thing like a pen knife or a cutter or something small, painted by her... it felt very normal as if we were a family.' Rounds of 'cat and mouse' were particularly enjoyed by the diminutive Tsar, who would target an agile, but obliging, engineer. The Tsarina herself occasionally joined in. Though not very limber, she probably did better than her friend, the portly Anya Vyrubova, who, according to Sablin, created much merriment as she 'lumbered about'.

Everyone on board took part in the games, even the *Standart*'s priest, Father Feodor Ivanovich Znamensky. Sablin was a great supporter of the canny priest who, as he reported: 'Had an excellent understanding of the environment in which he happened to be; he did not set any objectives and since the officers and the team always tried to sneak away from the services, he made them short and sweet.'

That evening, the parties dined on the British royal yacht. 'At 8.30 the two of us went to the *Victoria and Albert* to a state dinner,' noted the Tsar. Soon after the imperial couple's arrival, the King faced a dilemma. Who would accompany him into the dining room: the Tsarina or the Dowager? English protocol dictated that the sovereign's wife should precede the Dowager; but this might put the older lady's nose out of joint. However, if the Tsarina were forced into second place, she might well seize a welcome opportunity to duck out altogether. The King handled the situation with his usual bluff aplomb. Taking the arms of both ladies, he declared: 'Tonight I am going to enjoy the unique honour of taking two empresses into dinner.'

The lavish nine-course meal began with 'Tortue claire, Consommé froid' and ended with the slightly more prosaic 'Glace aux Pêches'. Headed with a royal crest and a picture of 'HMY *Victoria and Albert*', the menu further featured: 'Filets de Boeuf garnis à la Bouquetière', 'Dindonneaux et poulets à la broche' and, not least, 'Cailles froides à la Russe'.

Relishing his new position as a British admiral, the Tsar now returned the compliment, suggesting the King accept the title: Admiral of the Russian fleet. As Hardinge wrote: 'At official banquet on board *V and A*, King proposed Tsar's health as British Admiral of the Fleet and the British cruisers thundered an admiral's salute. The Tsar was pleased at the honour and countered the compliment by asking him to be an admiral "of our young and growing fleet".'

In fact, the young and growing Russian fleet comprised just one ship, the *Almaz*, now acting as a floating hotel for the Russian ministers. The rest of the fleet had been sunk at Tsushima, during the Russo-Japanese War. As Hardinge put it bluntly: 'The *Almaz* only existing representative'. The Tsar, as usual, recognised no awkwardness: 'I appointed Uncle Bertie an Admiral of our navy.'

Admiral Fisher was considered by some to be a troublesome presence at Reval. He was regarded with alarm by the Kaiser, who suspected him of poisoning the King's mind against Germany. There were fears, elsewhere, that he was urging Stolypin on to war, keen to build up land forces facing Germany.

At table, however, Fisher was more interested in carrying on his flirtation with the Tsar's sister, Olga. His success was such that the Grand Duchess was soon guffawing loudly.

H.M.Y. Victoria and Albert

Tortue claire.
Consommé froid.
—
Filets de Soles à la Joinville.
—
Cailles froides à la Russe.
—
Filets de Bœuf garnis à la Bouquetière.
—
Jambon au Champagne.
Dindonneaux et poulets à la Broche.
Salade de Romaine.
—
Asperges d' Argenteuil, Sauce Mousseuse.
—
Pains d' Ananas à la Créole.
Coupes Jacques.
—
Pailles au Parmesan.
—
Glace aux Pêches.

———

Reval.   10 Juin 1908.

The menu for the lavish nine-course dinner given in honour
of the imperial couple by Bertie on the royal yacht

As she explained: 'Admiral Fisher could tell the funniest stories and my laughter was known to carry far.' The King was eventually obliged to rebuke Fisher: 'Just remember you aren't a midshipman any longer.' Olga later gave a fond description of her riotous evening: 'At a dinner on board the *V und A*, I laughed so loudly that Uncle Bertie raised his head and asked Admiral Fisher to remember he was not in the guardroom. I felt dreadful... I had to wait until dinner was over and I could tell Uncle Bertie that it had all been my fault.' But the irrepressible Admiral had not finished. After dinner, he was intent on recapturing the romance of those dancing lessons in Karlsbad. The parties had barely settled themselves on deck, before Fisher approached Olga, bowing and offering her his arm. The couple then took their place in a grand circle, featuring the two monarchs and their ministers, and the orchestra struck up the waltz from the *Merry Widow*. As Olga was swung around by the handsome Admiral, she may have given a wistful thought to merry widows. There's no account of what her husband, or indeed Fisher's wife, thought of the revelry.

The King's exact thoughts are, equally, unknown, but Fisher felt he could gauge his audience, enthusing to his friend Reginald McKenna: 'I said to my sweet partner: "How about Siberia for me after this?" which sent her into hysterics... the Grand Duchess Olga felt herself like Herodias' daughter [Salome] as they formed a ring all round us while we danced! And my head wasn't wanted on a charger!'

When he had worn Olga out, Fisher proceeded to dance on his own. As the journalist W.T. Stead later wrote: '"Jacky" went on deck and by requests, which were commands, he brought down the house by dancing a hornpipe in approved nautical fashion.' Fisher was always keen to show off his steps. Three years before, he had pushed his luck by asking Queen Alexandra for a dance. 'Certainly not', came the reply.

Nonetheless, Olga was convinced that all the male members of the Russian party were won over by Fisher's antics. She wrote 'Sir John' a gushing letter: 'All our gentlemen – ministers, admirals and generals – were delighted with you, as you brought such an amount of frolic and jollity into their midst. They couldn't get over it and spoke about you and your dancing, anecdotes, etc, without end. I told them that, even if they tried their very hardest, they would never reach anywhere near your level. I shall never forget the last evening, when you entertained Victoria and me with your solo performance. I hadn't laughed so much for ages.'

Queen Alexandra may have turned down her opportunity to dance with Fisher, but she recognised his charm, noting wryly: 'He even succeeded in achieving the impossible by bringing a smile to the face of the Empress of Russia.' Fisher himself was proud of that particular achievement: 'They told me she [the Tsarina] had not laughed for two years.' On 12th June he wrote to his friend McKenna boasting of his progress with the Russian party; he admitted that the Tsar remained a little wary: 'The whole lot of them are now all dead-on for the Emperor coming to England but he said to one of them: "Don't let us hurry too much, we might spoil it".'

The Tsar gave the briefest description of the evening's merriment. There was no reference to his wife's rare smile: 'We talked for a long time, listened to the choruses again, singing from the sailboats. Olga danced with Admiral Fisher.'

Mossolov expressed his admiration, once again, for the generally convivial atmosphere: 'On board the *Victoria and Albert* things were done differently. After dinner the King and his august guests sat down in comfortable armchairs; coffee and liqueurs were served; an armchair was left vacant alongside each person of high rank and the officers with whom the King wanted to talk were invited to sit down in one of these chairs; after a fairly long conversation, the King would nod and his interlocutor would retire for somebody else to take his place.'

The evening concluded with fond farewells. 'The Emperor and Empress said goodbye to the King and we all shook hands warmly with the Russian suite and the next morning we left for England,' recalled Ponsonby. The Tsar took his leave, as he had done at Balmoral, without regrets: 'We said goodbye to Uncle Bertie, Aunt Alix and Victoria around 12 midnight and returned to our ship in the quiet of a bright night.'

Thursday 11th June
The Tsar's diary: 'The day was excellent.'

The parties went their separate ways. The *Victoria and Albert* weighed anchor in the early hours of the morning, arriving at Port Victoria three days later. The Tsar remained in good form, probably further buoyed up by the departure of the

British ships: 'At 3am the English ships weighed anchor and sailed out to sea. The roadstead was markedly empty.'

Passing mentions were made of work: 'Received Izvolsky's report'/'Received Stolypin after lunch'. Otherwise, the Tsar welcomed a return to the *Standart* idyll: 'Prayers were said on the occasion of Tatiana's birthday.' (The little Grand Duchess Tatiana had just turned 11). A farewell dinner followed with his mother, the Dowager; sister, Grand Duchess Olga; and brother-in-law, Grand Duke Peter: 'At 11pm we said goodbye to her [his mother], Olga and Petya.' The comforting bedtime routine was outlined by Sablin: 'Towards 12.30 on *Standart*, the sailor in charge of cabins would inform the watch: "His Majesty has deigned to go to bed".'

By the following day, the Tsar was basking in balaika music from the *Standart*'s own orchestra: an improvement, doubtless on the efforts of the Reval Musical Society: 'Weather was ideal but cool. We also weighed anchor at 10.30 and sailed out to sea. We cross over to Pikopas under the best conditions – 135 miles in eight and a half hours time. The sea was delightful… The balalaikas played during dinner.'

Sablin described the arrangements following the meeting: 'After departure of the British, *Standart* returned to Kronstandt from Reval. And Their Majesties left for Peterhof, promising that in the autumn we would be sailing as always but not for long because, on doctors' advice, the Empress wanted to undergo treatment in Nauheim, Germany, where the entire family was going in autumn.'

It is perhaps a measure of the Tsarina's general low spirits, that Spiridovich deemed 1908 one of her better years. He remembered her as being unusually happy during a subsequent sail through the fjords: 'There had been a particularly agreeable atmosphere that year in the fjords. The Empress's constant good mood, her appearance of good health, everyone's desire to please her, had created an exceedingly pleasant ambience, happy with the happiness of youth... When Alix happy, everybody happy.'

Admiral Fisher's verdict on the two-day meeting was ecstatic. As he wrote to McKenna: 'The visit has been a phenomenal triumph... the King has surpassed himself all round. Every blessed Russian of note he got quietly into his spider web and captured!' Hardinge was almost as enthusiastic: 'All my time at Reval spent talking to Stolypin and Izvolsky on foreign affairs... good progress made. Short conversations with the Tsar in best possible spirits.' He was apparently determined to overlook the Tsarina's tearful episode: 'There was no disguising the fact that the Emperor and Empress were extraordinarily happy in the company of their uncle and aunt.'

In her biography of Admiral Fisher, *Fisher's Face*, Jan Morris outlines the reasons behind the meeting: 'The purpose of the Reval meeting was to make sure that in another European war they would be allies rather than enemies and to reassure the nervous Tsar that he would not be alone if Germany attacked his territories.' Jane Ridley, Edward VII's biographer, describes its successful outcome: 'Reval achieved its aim of strengthening ties between Russia and Britain.' For his part, Spiridovich quoted a report in *The*

Times: 'Together with France, this [Anglo-Russian] entente will, from now on, work on consolidating general peace. The friendship between these three countries can only serve to strengthen each country.'

Russian newspapers referred to a 'feast of peace'. Hugh O'Beirne wrote buoyantly to the Foreign Secretary, Edward Grey, from St Petersburg, on 18th June: 'I have been assured, from many widely different quarters, of the excellent effect produced on Russian opinion by the Reval meeting... The King's toast to "the welfare above all" of this "great empire" produced, I know, the happiest impression, not only among politicians but also in court circles, where narrower views are apt to prevail.' Prince Orloff, the Tsar's principle aide-de-camp, told Fisher that the King: 'changed the atmosphere of Russian feelings towards England from suspicion to cordial trust'.

The writer Donald M. Wallace, who had been at Balmoral during the Romanovs' visit, might have welcomed Prince Orloff's comments about 'cordial trust' but he later revealed that he had no time for the man himself: '[Orloff], the fattest member of a corpulent family, is stolid and indolent.'

The meeting did not go down well in Germany. It would not have escaped the Kaiser's notice that there were no German journalists among the group of 40 special correspondents at Reval. He now complained of being 'encircled' by hostile neighbours: 'The King aims at war. I am to begin it so that he doesn't get the odium.'

Nicolson reiterated Grey's original claim, in Westminster, that the meeting was never intended to have a political element. 'The German press has often attributed great political importance to that visit, and has wished to have it believed that secret arrangements were reached which had for their object the "encircling" and isolation of Germany. There is no truth in this. The two sovereigns did not discuss politics at all and their meeting, with their respective families, was a strictly family reunion. Sir Charles Hardinge and M. Izvolsky had some conversations regarding Macedonia and other matters, but they were merely an interchange of views and nothing definite was concluded.' For all his talks with Stolypin, Izvolsky and the Tsar, Hardinge echoed Nicolson's view: 'The visit had largely a family character.'

Nonetheless it was partly as a result of the Reval meeting that, four months later, the Russo-English Chamber of Commerce was formed at St Petersburg, joined by leading members of the Duma and the Council of the British Empire, in the hope that the declining trade between the two countries would prosper.

While trade relations began to flourish, London enjoyed a respite from some of its Russian revolutionaries. Lenin had gone to settle in Switzerland, where he was joined, just before Christmas, by Prince Kropotkin, who was following doctor's instructions to take a break from the damp air of Bromley.

❧

That autumn, the Romanov children's new English tutor, Sydney Gibbes, made his first appearance at the Russian court. Priding himself on his discretion, Mr Gibbes revealed little of his first days with the two elder Grand Duchesses, Olga and Tatiana: though he did pay tribute to their decorum in not commenting when he forgot to put his tie on. Like Sablin, he took a particular shine to the third daughter, Maria: 'I took as my first lesson the two elder girls. They took their lessons together. Olga and Tatiana... Then I had the third daughter by herself... [Maria] was the most charming of all, the sweetest character and the greatest of them in artistic talent.' Mr Gibbes was unfazed by the Tsarina's frequent presence during his lessons. Indeed he gave a rapturous description of her: 'Not haughty in the ordinary sense, she never forgot her position, she looked queenly, but I was always at ease with her... she had a fresh complexion and beautiful hair and eyes. She gave you her hand with dignity mingled with shyness, which gave her a truly gracious air.' Apparently her large feet, which he also noted, did not detract from her dignity.

He was aware that his glowing view of the Tsarina was not widely shared in Russia; he laid the reason for her unpopularity squarely at Queen Victoria's door: 'I think that the cause of this must be attributed to the Empress's lack of a theatrical sense. The theatrical instinct is so deeply engrained in the Russian nature that one often feels that Russians act their lives rather than live them. This was completely foreign to the Empress's school of thought... which she had mostly acquired under the tutelage of her revered grandmother, Queen Victoria.'

Some months after enjoying the fjords, the Tsarina suffered another downturn, refusing to join her husband at their customary reception for the diplomatic corps at new year. This time the trouble was her nerves. Despite her frequent protest 'The peasants love us,' Alix had developed a fear of large gatherings. As Nicky told his cousin, Grand Duke Konstantin Konstantinovich: 'The Empress is very unwilling to receive, and is fearful of people, especially in crowds.'

Alexis was absent from the new year liturgy, at Tsarskoe Selo, following a fall. Grand Duke Konstantin recalled being told that the boy had 'inflammation of the knee joint'.

Of course, as long as the Tsarevich suffered from such inflammations, Rasputin would remain a welcome visitor in the royal household. In March 1909 the Tsarina wrote effusively to her daughters: 'I'm glad you had him [Rasputin] so long to yourselves, 1,000 kisses, Mama.' She instructed her eldest daughter, Olga: 'Remember above all to always be a good example to the little ones, then Our Friend [Rasputin] will be contented with you.' On the 26th April, the Tsar wrote in his diary: 'From 6 to 7.30 we saw Grigory [Rasputin] together with Olga. After dinner I had a go at billiards with Dmitri and in the evening sat for a while again with Grigory in the nursery.'

The young Grand Duchesses themselves were smitten, with the second daughter, Tatiana, writing to Rasputin: 'Without you it is so boring, so boring.' Maria was equally keen: 'As soon as I wake up in the morning, I take the gospel you gave me from under my pillow and kiss it... then I feel as though I am kissing you.' The youngest, Anastasia, added urgently: 'When are you coming? Come soon.' In June, Olga wrote to her father: 'My dear kind Papa. ... Grigory is coming to see us this evening. We are all so very happy that we will see him again.'

While the Romanovs communed with Grigory, their

Uncle Bertie had endured a challenging Mediterranean cruise with his wife and sister-in-law, the Dowager. Upon reaching Naples, the forceful sisters decided they wanted to visit Vesuvius.

Unbeknownst to the King, the Queen ordered donkeys to carry the party from the royal train to the mouth of the crater. Bertie, much put out and topping 16 stone, flatly refused to join the expedition, or even try to mount his donkey.

Half an hour after the party set off, accompanied by the redoubtable Ponsonby, a shrill whistle came from the train: Bertie was growing impatient. Ponsonby tried to persuade the sisters to turn back, but they were intent on reaching the crater. By the time the Queen relented, the Dowager, riding the fastest donkey, was a quarter of a mile ahead: 'a speck in the distance', as Ponsonby put it. He described his dismay as he set off after her: 'Trotting over indented larva on a donkey of uncertain habits was not amusing.' The Dowager was eventually persuaded to return, her speedy mount ensuring that she was first to reach the train. The King was by then, according to Ponsonby, 'boiling with rage'.

THE ISLE OF WIGHT

It was at the height of that summer, in 1909, that the Tsar, Tsarina and their five children arrived for their first family visit to Britain.

The visit was painstakingly choreographed to avoid provoking, once again, the radical factions. The Isle of Wight was selected as suitably discreet and remote: an island would offer 'Nicholas the Bloody' protection from the more excitable of his detractors. Sixty years before, in 1848, Queen Victoria herself had used the Isle of Wight as a safe haven when mob rule loomed on the mainland. The Chartist movement, demanding more political rights for working people in Britain, had reached a climax, with large demonstrations and a petition containing nearly six million signatures presented to the House of Commons.

It was agreed that the Romanovs would be permitted to moor the *Standart* off Cowes for three nights and three days. As at Reval, meetings with the King, Queen and various royal cousins, would take place largely on board the *Standart* and the *Victoria and Albert*. The British party would include the Prince of Wales, the Tsar's look-alike cousin and future King George V. The vexed question of whether the Tsar would be able to step ashore remained, for some time, unresolved.

The long-awaited visit to Britain got off to a bad start. All five children were seasick, obliged to retreat to a makeshift sickbay near the main mast, where there was less rocking. The seasickness had begun during some hefty swells on the way to their previous stop-off, in France. Sablin wrote that several desperate measures had failed, not least: 'a whole trunkful of special remedies from America'.

At one point, the sailors had resorted to hanging a special chair on springs for Tatiana, now aged 12, who was the worst hit. But the chair made her feel more ill. She felt queasy continually, even when the yacht was docked. As Sablin wrote wryly: 'The dear old nannies followed the Grand Duchesses with pails.' Andrei Derevenko, the sailor who looked after the little Tsarevich, held a fifth silver pail under the boy's chin while he 'fed the fish'.

As the *Standart* neared the pas du Calais, the sea calmed and the family sat down to dinner in the grand dining room. But they had barely started eating before the yacht began rocking again and the Tsarina and the children had to rush from the table. The Tsar did not suffer any sickness himself, but he was, predictably, rattled: 'The sovereign got up without having coffee,' recalled Sablin. 'Things started flying about, cabin crew rushed to save crockery and fasten the furniture. Huge ripples were coming from the Channel and we were awash… the sea was still raging and the ship was heaving severely.'

The Tsar steeled himself to stay up throughout the stormy night. As Sablin added: 'All the officers were on the top deck in emergency mode, and the Emperor went down to his cabin only at dawn.'

The Tsar alluded to the conditions in his diary: 'At 7pm we entered the English Channel and again there was a swell. During dinner the yacht swayed good enough in a belching sea, but it shook the ship even worse when at 9pm we dropped anchor in a turbulent sea around the Gris Nez [Grey Nose] lighthouse not far from Boulogne.'

The turbulence at sea was matched by a build-up of protest. In the weeks leading up to the visit, the Tsar had been repeatedly lambasted in the House of Commons for his ongoing poor record on civil liberties and state censorship. One MP denounced the Tsar's prospective visit as 'repulsive to multitudes of our people'. In Russia, he added, there was a 'vast amount of almost indescribable suffering'. It was pointed out that there was no sign of a let-up in the levels of repression and censorship – attention was drawn to the fact that prisoners in Russia now included some 237 deputies of the Duma and 400 editors of newspapers. The fiery Labour leader, Keir Hardie, who had objected so strongly to

The *Standart*, en route to Cowes, 1909

the Reval meeting, was back on the attack: 'People of this country are rising in indignation against the visit.'

Hardie's outburst led to an altercation between the King and the Home Secretary, Herbert Gladstone, son of the former Prime Minister. The younger Gladstone took it upon himself to give Hardie's speech a mild seal of approval: 'Mr Keir Hardie spoke on the whole with restraint.' The following day he received a furious response: 'The King CANNOT agree with his estimate of Keir Hardie's speech.' Gladstone hastily replied: 'In using the word "restraint" it was in a relative and personal sense. I look upon Mr Keir Hardie's attitude and views in the matter of the Tsar's visit as objectionable... what I wished to convey was that having regard to Mr Hardie's extreme views and his excitability and the expectation of a "scene" he did manage to keep himself under sufficient restraint.'

Outside the Commons, there was no shortage of 'scenes'. Radicals were holding meetings with increasing frequency and calls were being made for the Tsar's assassination. Questions were raised in the cabinet. As the Prime Minister, Herbert Asquith, reported on 16th June: 'Attention was called to some violent articles which have recently appeared in a Socialist newspaper called *Justice* and which might be construed as an incitement to the assassination of the Tsar on his approaching visit.'

The Foreign Secretary, Edward Grey, insisted that the protesters were no more than general trouble-makers. He wrote to Francis Knollys, on 25th July: 'It is I fear impossible to make any impression upon the extreme men who oppose the Tsar's visit. They want something about which to be violent, to force the more moderate men to be violent too.

They have chosen the Tsar's visit for this purpose and they will not discuss it on its merits.' Signatories to a 'Resolution of Protest' included Explosive Workers (Woolwich Workers Union, 36 Kingsdale Road, Plumstead) and Citizens of Rochdale and Ramsbottom Weavers, Winders and Warpers Association, 62 Stanley Street.

Additional questions were raised in the house: how many members of the Metropolitan Police were to be stationed on the Isle of Wight? Who was paying? Who was protecting Britain?

Days before the visit, hundreds of protesters joined Keir Hardie for a demonstration in Trafalgar Square. The British and Russian authorities played it down, with Hardinge insisting that the protest comprised no more than: 'five hundred Frenchmen, six hundred German waiters, a few Russian Jews and Italian ice vendors'.

Benckendorff assured Izvolsky, equally breezily, that there were barely 300 English Socialists present at the rally. The rest, he claimed, were simply 'badauds' (idlers). There seemed to be little trace of Prince Kropotkin, who had been so ready with his 'Down with the Romanovs' note, or Burtsev, whose publication had once advocated the Tsar's assassination. Benckendorff added that the British newspapers had been unimpressed: 'La presse ne s'en est occupé qu'à peine.'

Indeed, in an effort to diffuse tension, the press was, at this stage, repeating assurances that the Tsar and the King would each play host to the other on their yachts. The Tsar, it was stressed, would not set foot on British soil.

Monday 2nd August
From the diary of Georgie, the Prince of Wales: 'Dear Nicky, looking so well, and Alicky too'.

In a slight echo of the 'dreich and misty' weather in Scotland, in 1896, the day of the arrival was described by the *Isle of Wight County Press* as 'dull and menacing'.

The poor conditions did nothing to dampen public interest. Thousands of stout-hearted spectators collected on the wind-swept shoreline to see the massive gathering of ships and boats, not least the British Naval Fleet: the spectacle enhanced by the roar of cannonfire, as Russian and British battleships exchanged greetings.

Private yachts and excursion boats crowded into the choppy Solent, vying for closer views, while hardy journalists ventured out on steamboats. The *Isle of Wight County Press* trumpeted: 'It is safe to say a more brilliant assembly of fashionable people has never been seen at Cowes... some exquisite toilettes were seen.'

The mood aboard the *Standart* that morning, before the crossing to the Isle of Wight, had not been good. The children should have been excited, not least at the prospect of meeting some of their cousins for the first time. Their stop-over at Cherbourg had, in the end, proved a success; they had all received lavish presents, not least 12 miniature rifles for the little Tsarevich. But there were still some 75 miles to go before they reached their destination. And, as Spiridovich wrote: 'The ladies on board the *Standart* were upset at having to go through the discomfort of the crossing again.'

Ladies' misgivings, however, were not going to disrupt

tight schedules. The *Standart* weighed anchor at 7am sharp: exactly an hour later, cannons were fired, as the French squadron escort was replaced by three British Dreadnoughts and several torpedo boats. A substantial Russian escort, already in place, comprised the Dowager's yacht, the *Polar Star*, two destroyers and two cruisers. As the convoy set off, the British ships allowed the *Standart* to pass, before forming a protective semi-circle behind her. Conditions continued to be unpromising: 'the sky cloudy and the sea gloomy', wrote Spiridovich. The Tsarina and her daughters' worst fears were borne out as they endured several hours of their dreaded discomfort. Even the imperturbable Georgie's diary contains references to a 'strongish breeze from the north'. Smudges of smoke from the three Dreadnoughts – *Invincible*, *Inflexible* and *Indomitable* – were seen from the Isle of Wight at around 11.30.

The imperial couple were both familiar with the Isle of Wight. The Tsarina had enjoyed many childhood holidays at Osborne, and her husband had come to share her enthusiasm, when he visited following his betrothal in 1894, writing exuberantly to Queen Victoria: 'My dearest Grandmama, I loved Osborne so much and was too delighted when you asked me to spend with you the last five days there!' It had not, in fact, been his first visit. In his diary, in 1894, he had referred, in passing, to a previous visit to Osborne, as a child: 'It is strange to think that I stayed here 21 years ago, but almost do not remember anything. The view from the windows on to the sound and to the other side is surprisingly beautiful!' His admission of memory failure elicited a sympathetic exclamation from his fiancée: 'Sweety dear!'

The young Grand Duchesses and the little Tsarevich were, however, being introduced to England for the first time. As they emerged from their heavily blanketed den, they must have been excited by the sight of the surrounding boats and struck by the numbers of onlookers. But their initial impressions would have been clouded by the pervasive gloom. As the Tsar wrote in his diary: 'Towards morning the yacht began to rock back and forth and crack up in the cabins. The day was grey and tedious.'

The Tsar's head of security, Spiridovich, retained a bleak memory of the moment the *Standart* reached Cowes: 'Here, the morning was even more unpleasant. A cold wind was blowing. The sea was inhospitable.'

⚜

The hardy crowd awaiting them would have been unaware of the exact choreography, but it was known that the King would be on the *Victoria and Albert*, ready to meet the Tsar. Those stalwarts watching from the shore would only be able to make out blurred figures, and unable to identify the principal characters – the Queen, the Tsarina and the Prince of Wales – without powerful binoculars.

Those braving the sea had a better chance of catching the finer details, such as the British royals boarding a smart launcher for the 200-yard transfer to the *Standart* and the 68-year-old King striding, in first place, up the gangway. The *County Press* described the British royal standard flag being hoisted slowly while: 'The two monarchs embraced with great affection'. There were references to the King and Queen Alexandra 'cordially saluting' the Tsarina. The young Grand Duchesses, it was reported, wore white gowns and huge picture hats. All five children were putting up a good front as they coped with ongoing sea swells: 'The imperial children were presented and formed an interesting portion of a happy domestic picture.'

One particularly captivating sight would have been the Tsar being reunited with his doppelgänger cousin, Georgie. The *Standart* officer Sablin found it hard to believe the extent of the resemblance: 'They looked so much alike that we could hardly distinguish them.'

The King had squeezed into a Russian admiral's uniform, while the Tsar dressed as a British admiral of the fleet. Later the Tsar would also appoint Georgie an Admiral in the Russian navy. The Tsar's reference to his costume may carry a slight hint of complaint: 'I stayed in the English admiral's uniform for six hours.'

Few would have guessed that the King and the Tsar were both, in fact, reluctant players in the pageant. For all their pleasantries at Reval, the Tsar never quite discarded his reservations about his overbearing uncle. He had to be cajoled into the Cowes visit by Izvolsky, having been anxious about antagonising the leaders of other European countries, not least the touchy Kaiser. One of his favourite court officials, Count Fredericks, had insisted, additionally, that Britain could never be a loyal ally. Despite his gloomy prognosis, the lavishly moustached Fredericks, then aged 70, had dutifully attended Reval and was now present at the Isle of Wight. The Count once blotted his copybook at court by failing to introduce the Tsar and a visitor, leaving both parties languishing in different rooms.

The Tsar knew only too well how upsetting the visit

Nicky with Georgie, his doppelgänger cousin

would be for Alix. With all her happy memories of Osborne, she would face endless painful reminders of her beloved grandmother. Queen Victoria had once written to the Tsar of her close relationship with Alix: 'As she has no parents, I feel I am the only person who can really be answerable for her. All her dear sisters after their beloved mother's death look to me as their second mother, but they still had their dear father... Now poor dear Alicky is an orphan and has no one but me at all in that position.'

The Romanovs' itinerary over the next few days was not generally known and may even have been undecided. But there were newspaper reports insisting that the Tsarina would visit the 17th-century Barton Manor, next to Osborne House, and her grandmother's church, St Mildred's, at Whippingham. In the event, though she visited Barton Manor, she never managed to see the church.

The King, meanwhile, never changed his poor opinion of his Russian nephew, complaining, in private, that he was: 'deplorably immature, unsophisticated and reactionary'. Though he was fond of the Tsarina, he had had no compunction about offending her at their last meeting: he must have known how hurtful she would have found his comments about her daughters' accents.

His wife, Queen Alexandra, had mixed feelings regarding the Tsarina. Her dry mention of Alix's rare smile, during Admiral Fisher's antics at Reval, reveals what she thought of her niece's dour temperament. She would have been aware of the ever-increasing tension between the Tsarina and her sister, the Dowager.

The central argument between the two women now revolved around the Tsarina's weakness for so-called 'holy fools', the most recent being 'Our Friend' Rasputin.

By the summer of 1909, Rasputin's visits to the palace were increasing as his reputation for drinking and womanising grew worse. Horrified courtiers and servants might have been reassured had they known of Rasputin's role as a healer, but Alexis's illness was kept secret, even from his relations: the Tsar's own sister, Xenia, was not told about it until 1912, by which time the boy was eight.

Shortly before the Isle of Wight trip, Rasputin had sent an intimate, if slightly random, telegram: 'Dear little children! Thank you for remembering me, for your sweet words, for your pure heart and your love for the people of God. Love the whole of God's nature, the whole of his creation, in particular this earth. The mother of God was always occupied with flowers and needlework.'

The Dowager would undoubtedly have shared her suspicion of Rasputin, 'that dubious individual', with her sister Queen Alexandra. The Tsarina, looking back on the visit to Cowes in a letter, paid tribute to the King: 'Dear uncle' had been 'most kind and attentive'. But there was no mention of her aunt.

⚜

While the royal parties put their efforts into 'cordial salutations', the authorities stepped up elaborate security arrangements. On the day of the Romanovs' arrival at the Isle of Wight, 70 MPs and two bishops made formal complaints. Keir Hardie said he was glad that 'contamination' from the visit was being contained at Cowes. The Tsar's yacht, he added, would be guarded 'like a plague spot'.

Queen Alexandra and the Tsarina

The countryside around Cowes was, indeed, teeming with Russian and British police. Patrolling cyclists raced through the leafy lanes, while Russian secret agents hung around in pairs, cursorily disguised in yachting caps. Emissaries from Scotland Yard and St Petersburg were stationed at Southampton, Portsmouth, Lymington and Bournemouth. Visitors arriving at the pier heads of Ryde, Seaview, Sandown, Shanklin, Ventnor, Alum and Totland Bays were scrutinised and some turned away. The island faced unprecedented numbers, some 12,000 visitors arriving over just a couple of days, at the Victoria Pier.

The *County Press* made the most of the excitement: 'The

Scotland Yard officers are, of course, fully acquainted with the movements in this country of the Russian and other foreign revolutionaries, and the few suspects of this connection who arrived at the yachting capital were promptly warned away.' The *Isle of Wight Times* reported: 'The local police frankly confess that they have never before had to deal with anything so comprehensive and complete as the scheme of protection for the Tsar, nor do they believe that an organisation to equal it has ever been formed in England.'

Pleasure launches circling both royal yachts were kept at bay by aggressive little Russian picket boats. Several were chased off and one of them was towed away by a torpedo boat. The journalist Henry Lucy felt that the security put a dampener on the occasion: 'The reception of the Tsar… was hopelessly depressed by the circumstance that, to put the matter bluntly, he shrank from setting his foot ashore… though all the resources of Scotland Yard, reinforced by a contingent of Russian secret police, familiar with the individuality of anarchists, had been invoked to keep murderous hands off, it was felt undesirable for His Majesty to land.'

One of the British party, Lord Suffield, had been to Russia and met Tsar Alexander II, who had later been assassinated. Even he was horrified by the security: 'Everybody seemed to be in fear for the poor hunted Tsar. I do not know how any man can submit to such thraldom; it is too big a price to pay for being a potentate!'

The first business conducted on board the *Standart* was, appropriately, a meeting of the heads of security. The Isle of Wight's Chief Constable, Captain H.G. Adams Connor, was in consultation with the Chief Commissioner of the Metropolitan Police, Sir Edward Henry. Throughout the visit, finer points regarding security could be discussed and amended, thanks to special telegraph and telephone cable laid down between the shore and the royal yachts. The *Standart* had her own telegraph office on board. The *County Press* recorded the Cowes post office as having: 'an unprecedented amount of business. It had been obliged to take on extra staff, largely augmented from London and other large centres.'

After the security chiefs came the diplomats, headed by the Russian Ambassador, Count Benckendorff. Throughout July, he had been exchanging letters with Knollys, containing the inevitable lists of prospective royal guests and their attendants. Further lists gave details of the recipients of various awards.

Benckendorff, by then 60, was distinguished-looking, tall and thin, with a long, lugubrious face and monocle. His moustaches were shorter than Izvolsky's but equally painstakingly curled. He had been curiously unenthusiastic about the visit. In a letter to Izvolsky, he wrote: 'Le Roi est ENCHANTE de voir l'Empereur chez lui'. But he proceeded to complain about the expense of the accommodation, insisting that Cowes had: 'un seul hotel à peu près propre', namely the Gloster Hotel.

The Ambassador was later described by Donald M. Wallace, who had been at Balmoral and was now extra-groom-in-waiting to the King, as generally 'uneasy and anxious'. Wallace added that the great Izvolsky, also, seemed to let his standards slip, appearing: 'not at all in high spirits'.

⚜

After a relatively brisk 20-minute reunion, the royal parties were transferred from the *Standart* to the *Victoria and Albert*. The King's Lord Chamberlain, the 6th Earl Spencer, recorded events at the Isle of White in his diary. Then 54, Spencer had drooping eyelids that lent him a rather supercilious expression. He was preoccupied with his dress and the day of the Tsar's arrival began badly: 'My new serge not a success with the King'.

But his subsequent presentation to the imperial couple went swimmingly; he proudly noted his progress with the reticent Tsarina: 'Empress very civil to me... Remembered the Windsor visit; talked about her children'. The Windsor visit would have been a reference to Alix's stay with her grandmother in 1894.

⚜

Luncheon was served, surprisingly late, at 2pm. The King escorted his niece, the Tsarina, to the table, while the Tsar accompanied his aunt, Queen Alexandra. No formal toasts were proposed, but the King raised his glass to the health of the imperial couple.

After lunch, the Tsar was besieged by British dignitaries, among them the Prime Minister, Herbert Asquith, the First Lord of the Admiralty and Fisher's correspondent, Reginald McKenna, and finally Edward Grey, who he had once insisted he was keen to meet. Benckendorff watched with misgivings, aware that the Tsar failed to impress the British statesmen, coming across as an 'entirely unaffected but well-informed country gentleman'. The future Edward VIII, then a boy of 15, agreed. He later wrote: 'I do not recall him [the Tsar] as a man of marked personality.'

Benckendorff had become convinced that the Tsar was outclassed by the King. Confiding his grim thoughts to a relation, he was perhaps over-generous in his list of the King's qualities: 'His skill, his tact, his aptitude to avoid quite effortlessly saying a foolish thing... and then to compare, that's what hurts.'

During his six years as Ambassador, Benckendorff had frequently found himself discomforted by his countrymen. He became wary of Russian theatrical events, anxious that performers might overdo their patriotism. In a letter to his wife, he described his rising tension during a concert at the London Colisseum: 'A balalaika plays "Rule Britannia" – the audience ecstatic. "God save the King"... I was wondering what the devil is going to happen next. I am sitting very much in the public view. I am getting worried. The orchestra strike up "God save the Tsar"...' His worries, on this occasion, were unfounded: the audience applauded politely.

At 3.20pm, the *Victoria and Albert* weighed anchor, in preparation for a review of the British fleet, accompanied by the *Standart*, the *Polar Star*, two Russian cruisers and two Russian destroyers. Twenty-eight admirals presided over a fleet comprising 24 battleships, 16 armoured cruisers, 48 destroyers and well over 50 other vessels of war, all arranged in three long lines.

The King and the Tsar stood side by side on the saloon deck of the *Victoria and Albert*, acknowledging cheers from British and Russian sailors. One photograph of the event, taken on the *Lord Nelson*, shows the somewhat choreographed nature of the cheering: the sailors, standing erect on the top deck next to the railings, evenly spaced, each with right hand raised waving a cap.

The Russian head of security, Spiridovich, was overwhelmed by the sight: 'Three rows of massive warships and several rows of smaller ships stretched in parallel lines in Spithead harbour and disappeared out towards Cowes... one enormously impressive force, defying reality, a complete vision of grandeur.' There was no let-up from the squally conditions, but, as Spiridovich wrote, the ships were restrained by their moorings 'like immense spindles placed between the steel giants by an almighty hand'. Even Sablin was entranced: 'The scene was majestic and awesome. What power, what brilliance!'

The fleet was almost too glorious. As Spiridovich added: 'It was not without an element of jealousy that we admired the splendid scene. If only we had something like this!' Donald M. Wallace recalled Admiral Konstantine Nilov's discomfort. The Admiral, he wrote, was: 'depressed that the British navy was better than the Russians'... The magnificent British fleet at Cowes made him think of the condition of the Russian navy, which he described to me as "deplorable"... A navy recruit may never have seen the sea in his life.... [there was a] general indifference to the Russian navy and higher posts [were] not always filled satisfactorily.'

Admiral Fisher was unable to resist ramming the point home: 'I told the Emperor it was a fine avenue! – 18 miles

Czar & King Edward on Board the
Victoria and Albert. Cheering from
the Lord Nelson as the Monarchs passed. 1910

The Tsar and Edward VII on board the *Victoria and Albert,*
acknowledging cheers from British and Russian sailors

of ships – the most powerful in the world and none of
them more than ten years old!'

In fact, the day before, during the welcome to the King,
the Royal Navy had suffered a serious accident when a
cannon backfired on HMS *Temeraire*. An able seaman died
after part of his left arm was shot away; while two ordinary seaman suffered injuries to the face and hands. All
three had been taken to the Royal Naval Hospital at Haslar.
The *County Press* reported: 'The King, to whom news of the
accident was communicated, expressed great concern, made
sympathetic inquiries and asked to be kept informed of the
progress of the sufferers.'

The review of the fleet was barely under way before the Russians underwent a humiliating setback when their cruiser, *Rurik*, nearly collided with another ship. The *Rurik* was already sullied by her links to one of the previous year's assassination plots. The shady Azev had been involved in the plan, scheduled to take place months after the Reval visit.

Presently, the *Standart* herself ran into difficulties, proving less nifty than the *Victoria and Albert*, which was very fast and, being smaller than the *Standart*, more manoeuverable – 'Chagin [the Admiral] had to reverse one of the engines, trying to stay in line with the English,' wrote Sablin.

Lord Suffield, on board the *Victoria and Albert*, had already been put out by the excessive security. He now saw mishaps galore: 'I felt quite bewildered as we passed up and down the lines of battleships in the midst of unprecedented turmoil; the pomp and circumstance of everything really seemed tiresome and the firing of salutes merely a great waste of valuable powder!'

The journalist Henry Lucy, however, was cheered by the display: 'The effect came as near as landsmen are likely to witness to the scene of actual battle. At first the smoke from the guns curling slowly round the ships was pierced by the sunlight streaming through. As the firing went on the cloud thickened, till, before the yacht carrying Caesar and his fortunes had sped a mile, she and he were lost in the smoke that bridged the broad avenue.' Caesar, coincidentally, was the name of Edward VII's dog, then on board the *Victoria and Albert*. The terrier was not a favourite of his wife. 'Horrid little dog', she would complain, days after her husband's death.

The windswept spectators must have been relieved when the review of the fleet was finally over. 'Favoured guests were taken ashore to Cowes, where they arrived in a bedraggled and otherwise pitiful condition,' wrote Henry Lucy,

During the late afternoon, several Russian courtiers grew intent on going ashore. 'None of us knew why we had been in such a hurry to disembark,' recalled Spiridovich. 'After all, we really didn't have any immediate tasks on landing.' But their eagerness did not stop them agonising about their appearance. They wanted to look like English gentlemen but so far their efforts had been rather hit-and-miss. Spiridovich recalled: 'Some of these military men tried to adapt to civilian clothing, to which they were not accustomed, and appear like real gentlemen. Unfortunately, they were not very successful at this and every so often one could see looks of amusement from our hosts.

'One of our party spent his time rolling up and down his trousers in an effort to follow the latest fashion trends. Finally, seeing that he was only crumpling his clothing, he gave up any further attempt and resigned himself to wearing trousers without any creases. But how shameful! What will the English say? Oh that damn tailor.'

Spirodovich's party faced further difficulties when their motorboat collided with a mysterious underwater obstacle. The accident happened after a high-handed Russian prince ordered the boat's helmsman to ignore guiding markers in the sea. According to Spirodovich, the helmsman tried to argue, but had been shouted down by the Prince. 'We veered out in a straight line for a few seconds, then heard a dreadful crash, and our boat stopped... We went backwards and forwards a few times before we were finally able to extricate ourselves.'

Arriving at Cowes a few minutes later, the Russian courtiers found themselves being stared at by a large crowd. Had they failed to look sufficiently like English gentlemen? It was impossible to tell. Spiriodivich was, however, gratified by the crowd's fascination: 'They looked at us curiously, admiring the smart young sailors from the guard crew, who indeed looked magnificent in their imperial navy uniforms.' Spiridovich himself was, at this point, a youthful and dapper 36.

The party paraded up and down the High Street. One crew member practised English phrases he had learnt at the Berlitz School in St Petersburg. He was mortified when an Englishwoman simply gawped at him, baffled, before replying in stilted French: 'Sorry, but I don't speak Russian.'

As supply officer for the *Standart*, Sabin was obliged to explore the shops at Cowes. He never made any bones about preferring France – 'beautiful country, with hearty hospitality' – to England. But his discovery of the English bank holiday was the last straw: 'All commercial establishments in the country are closed and you cannot change any letter of credit or buy a pound of bread.' In France, it had been very different: 'In spite of being Sunday, the banks were open to us. We not only exchanged letters of credit but were also welcomed with fine wine in the company of charming employees, representing the beautiful half of the human race [women].'

Sablin was disappointed by the consul in Cowes. 'He turned out to be an elderly Englishman who could not come out to meet me.... People were saying he was so old that he could not get out of bed or someone even said he had died long ago and the consular affairs were managed by his wife and son. The consul's age was evident from the letters in which he wrote market prices and various certificates.'

Interestingly the police were still unsure of the Tsar and Tsarina's itinerary. It was emerging that earlier press reports, denying that the Tsar would land, were not set in stone. Spiridovich recalled meeting police representatives and speaking to them about what further security would be necessary if 'Their Majesties' ever came ashore.

The Prince of Wales, Georgie, took the early evening easily: '6pm, read and rested, as I was pretty tired after standing about all day.'

That first night, both royal families dined on board the *Victoria and Albert*. Forty-four guests sat at one long table, decorated with red roses and gold centre pieces. The King sat in the middle, with the Tsarina on his right. The Tsar was immediately opposite, with Queen Alexandra on his right. Dignitaries included the Crown Prince and crown Princess of Sweden, Herbert Asquith, Edward Grey and, naturally, Admiral Fisher, who kept a low profile, perhaps feeling the absence of his Grand Duchess Olga. Georgie recorded the few he saw as guests of note: 'Nicky and Alicky and Russian suite',

Sablin proved predictably out of sorts, describing the atmosphere at dinner as: 'characterised by stiffness and tension'. There was no mention here of the King's subtle humour or charming sweetness. Was the loyal Sablin over-sensitive to the pressures on the imperial couple? The Tsar would have had mixed feelings about all the social challenges, while the Tsarina was, once again, unwell. This time, it was not her legs letting her down, but her head. She was suffering, as her husband had, from neuralgia. Donald M. Wallace recalled being told by one of her ladies-in-waiting that the Tsarina had been afflicted with: 'facial neuralgia which prevented her from sleeping well at night'. Wallace shared Sablin's view of the atmosphere, registering the unease of his neighbour, Benckendorff: 'He always sat silent, glancing up and down the table, as if looking for somebody he could not find.'

Thankfully, Sablin rallied sufficiently to appreciate the food, or, as he put it, 'the remarkable sophistication and refinement of the cuisine'. The exotic menu included: 'Cailles Froides à la Muscovite', 'Timbales de Poires à la Siberienne' and 'Glace à la Czarine'. The musical entertainment featured a band from Portsmouth playing a piece from Tchaikovsky's *Eugene Onegin*, a xylophone solo called 'Le Jongleur' and Squire's 'The Merry Nigger'.

The King's speech was, once again, off the cuff: 'I am proud to welcome you both to British waters... Your Majesty, as well as my dear niece, are no strangers to England, especially to the Isle of Wight and I trust your memory will carry you back to years ago, when the hospitality of my beloved mother was extended to you both... I trust that Your Majesty will never look upon these ships as symbols of war, but, on the contrary, as a protection to our coasts and commerce and, above all for upholding the interests of peace.'

The Tsar's more elaborate speech was, needless to say, carefully prepared: 'I take great pleasure in expressing my heartiest thanks for the kind words with which Your Majesty has been pleased to welcome the Empress and myself in British water. The magnificent review which I witnessed today bears full testimony to England's great-ness.... Fifteen years have passed since last I came to Cowes. I shall ever bear in mind the happy days spent with your beloved and venerated mother, Queen Victoria, and the affection she bestowed upon me, as upon the Empress, her granddaughter.'

Georgie wrote agreeably in his diary: 'Papa proposed Nicky's health which he answered. Very nice speeches.' Earl Spencer was equally impressed by the King: 'Excellent speech. Rather moved....', but dismissive of the Tsar: 'The Emperor read his reply.'

If Izvolsky was generally down in the mouth, he would have been cheered by references, in both speeches, to a recent visit to Britain by delegates from the Russian parliament. The Duma delegates had been received, according to Benckendorff, 'warmly but tactfully'. Another reason to be cheerful was the prospect of a weekend at a grand country estate with the aristocratic Savile family. Izvolsky had a special relationship with Lady Savile, to whom he had written on 22nd July: 'It is awfully kind of you to ask me to Rufford Abbey and I am afraid I cannot resist the temptation to see you in your beautiful home.... a letter will find me... on 2nd August at Cowes, on board the

The *Polar Star* on which Izvolsky sailed as part of
the imperial entourage

Russian imperial yacht *Polar Star*...

'I cannot tell you how I look forward to my visit at
Rufford Abbey and to a nice long talk with you. I saw
so little of you during my last stay in England and this is
such a pleasant way of meeting you. Please convey my best
thanks to Lord Savile and believe me yours ever, sincerely,
Izvolsky.'

Donald M. Wallace attributed Izvolsky's low mood on
the Isle of Wight to a lack of such glittering female company:
'Izvolsky enjoys the admiration of charming fashionable
ladies and he did not receive at Cowes quite as much of that
stimulant as he would have liked... one or two fair beings
found him positively unsympathetic and ugly and perhaps
did not entirely succeed in concealing this feeling... he was
certainly morose.'

Spirodivich, who sailed with Izvolsky on the *Polar Star*
was struck by the minister's tension, describing him as:
'haughty and inscrutable. It was as if he were trying hard to
contain himself and would soon spill all the secrets he had.'

After dinner, members of the Russian embassy and

Cowes. Tuesday
August 3rd

Dear Lady Savile. Best thanks for your two kind notes. I shall follow your instructions and arrive at Newark on Saturday, 8th August at 6. p. m. It shall be such a pleasure to see you. Yours sincerely Isvolsky

The Lady Savile
Rufford Abbey
Ollerton.
Notts.

Let me know whether this suits you. I sail from here on Sunday next and a letter will find me on July 31st and August 1st at Cherbourg, and on August 2nd at Cowes, on board the Russian Imperial Yacht "Polar Star". On August 5th I shall be in London, Russian Embassy.

I cannot tell you how I look forward to my visit at Rufford Abbey

and to a nice long talk with you. I saw so little of you during my last stay in England and this is such a pleasant way of meeting you. Please convey my best thanks to Lord Savile and believe me Yours ever sincerely

Isvolsky.

Izvolsky's letter to Lady Savile

Russian naval captains were invited to circulate. Lord Suffield was more enthusiastic about the dinner than he had been about the review. 'We had a great dinner party... and the King took me by the arm, as he always did, and presented me once more to the Emperor of all the Russias, telling him how often I had been in his country, and so on. The Tsar was very gracious and kind.' Izvolsky cast aside his moroseness for a while, enjoying his reunion with the King. The pair discussed Sherwood Forest and the daring deeds of Robin Hood.

By the time Lord Suffield and several notables returned to their pier, the harbour master had locked up and gone to bed. Suffield, then 79 years old, had to be hoisted over the gates by the Commodore and the Duke of Leeds. But he was made of strong stuff; one of his ancestors had shot a bear in Russia and had it stuffed. It stood for years – most likely at the family's Gunton estate in Norfolk – with its paws outstretched, proffering food trays.

After dark, the royal yachts, the fleet and 150 other vessels, were lit up. Spiridovich was enraptured: 'As if turned on by a magic switch, the entire English fleet was illuminated with electric lights along the main lines of vessels. The silver outlines of the sea giants stood out against the liquid darkness of the night. As we looked further out in the distance, the illuminated spectres appeared smaller and smaller, and the last of them, those furthest away, only displayed thin threads of silver. This colossal, immobile stationary fleet looked like something out of a fairytale.' One British observer wrote: 'The riding lights and lanterns gleamed and shone like glow-worms against the onyx water.'

Grandees gazed in awe at the spectacle from their own splendid yachts. Nonie May Leeds, the widow of an American tinplate millionaire, was later hailed by *The New York Times* as Cowes' biggest spender of 1909. She was shelling out £500 a day (over £40,000 in today's money) for her 'floating palace', *Margarita*. Among her guests was Lady Muriel Paget, who would later move to St Petersburg to set up the Anglo-Russian hospital. Sablin enjoyed a rare moment of unbridled excitement, gazing at the ships through a telescope: 'And the boats! Steam vessels, sailing boats, big ocean liners from America'.

The famously acquisitive Princess of Wales, May, enjoyed rich pickings that day. She enthused in her diary that the Tsarina had given her a trinket, the anchor of St Catherine, 'which for years I had wanted to have!!!' Georgie's entry was characteristically sparse: 'Beautiful night but rather cold. Bed at 11.30'. Earl Spencer closed his diary with: 'My cabin at 11.45… the air is refreshing though today has been rather trying for one's feet.'

Tuesday 3rd August
The Princess of Wales, May, wrote in her diary: 'Went to… Osborne Bay to meet the charming little Russian children. Picked up shells with them on the beach.'

By daybreak the following morning, the fleet had completely

disappeared. An awe-struck Spiridovich wrote: 'Noiselessly, without anyone noticing, this vast fleet had spirited itself out of port during the night. You had to be a true sailor to appreciate the virtuosity of such a manoeuvre.'

The weather had improved. The *County Press* reported: 'Tuesday turned out to be a very much better day. There was a nice northerly sailing breeze and the day was much warmer and brighter than the bank holiday had been.' Spiridovich concurred: 'The weather was glorious, clear and hot, with a light breeze blowing.'

The Tsar met officers of the Royal Scots Greys before breakfast, thoughtfully insisting they remove their thick bearskin hats. As Sablin recounted: 'After a few minutes the sovereign asked all the officers to remove them, which was a small deviation from the strict British regulations: the officers of the regiment wear them on their heads for hours, but never complain!'

Later, as Sablin watched the King eating breakfast with the Tsar, he felt, once again, that 'Uncle Eddie' was being patronising towards his nephew. He preferred Georgie's manner towards the Tsar, noting that the young men's physical resemblance was matched by similarities in character: 'Edward VII was in good spirits and made charming jokes. But yet again a sense of superiority and some condescension towards our good-natured and shy Emperor was evident. But the Prince of Wales, the future King, was very heartfelt towards the sovereign, having, apparently, the same nature as his cousin.'

Sablin could not have known how the cousins' friendship was destined to be tested in the years to come.

The Tsar received several delegations, after which the imperial couple watched the royal yacht squadron races with the King and Queen. At some point, Nicky and Georgie sailed together on the racing cutter, *Britannia*. Among their competitors was the *Shamrock*, owned by the 'tea king' (as Sablin called him) Sir Thomas Lipton. Sablin recalled: 'For such races, the Prince of Wales dressed as a simple sailor, with his cap without a visor, bearing a ribbon with *Britannia* on it. The Emperor was wearing a marine guard's service jacket.'

The wind now began to pick up. Even Georgie was struck: 'There was a fair breeze... and it is not very warm.' Sablin gave a graphic report: 'Heave, heave was coming from every yacht. *Britannia* was heeling a lot, with the floor deck under the water, and everyone was on it, leaning with their feet firmly against the bulwarks. But *Britannia* did not take the first prize.'

Sablin added: 'The Emperor was not very fond of sailing; nevertheless, he returned feeling very lively and saying that he was very impressed. It was [only] the second time in my ten years of service on the *Standart* when the Emperor was on a boat under sail.'

So buoyed up was the Tsar by his sailing that he didn't appear to notice a further blow to the morale of the Russian navy. 'Unfortunately not a single Russian yacht was taking part, even though we had excellent international racers and yachts,' complained Sablin.

At 12pm the Tsar and Tsarina boarded *Britannia* for what Spencer, unusually chirpily, referred to as a 'delightful

cruise towards Stokes Bay'. The Tsar was almost as enthusiastic: 'It was pleasant to sit down and breathe in the fresh
air.' Spencer complained that the sun was 'fearfully hot',
but he managed more conversation with the Tsarina: 'Great
deal of talk to the Empress'.

The Tsarina was not a great one for enjoying herself: four
days of relentless entertainment would have been especially
taxing. But during this particular cruise she was photographed smiling with uncharacteristic abandon, leaning
boldly towards her cousin, Princess Victoria. The pair, who
had met at Balmoral as well as at Reval, are chatting on
deck: Victoria looks as if she is telling a story, while the
Tsarina laughs.

On a second occasion, she floored King Edward's

Bertie with Queen Alexandra on deck

mistress, Alice Keppel, with a further burst of exuberance. By 1909, Mrs Keppel had become Bertie's frequent companion and confidante. After he died, Mrs Keppel told Lord Rosebery that: 'the King showed her every letter he received within minutes of receiving it'. She had chestnut hair and a large bust; Lady Lytton dismissed her as 'a rather coarse type of woman'.

Mrs Keppel noticed the Tsarina's 'frigid calm' on deck. She followed the Tsarina downstairs to a suite of rooms after receiving an unexpected invitation. Upon reaching the suite, she found that her hostess completely changed character: 'There was a sudden lightening of the atmosphere and the Tsarina became almost skittish – "Tell me, my dear, where do YOU get your knitting wool?"'

On their way back from the cruise, the imperial couple paid a brief visit to the exiled French Empress Eugenie, who was installed on her own steam yacht, *Thistle*. The Empress had lived in exile in Farnborough, in Hampshire, since the overthrow of her husband, Napoleon III, in 1870. The Tsar had, dined with her and Queen Victoria at Windsor, in 1894. According to Sablin, meetings with the Empress had to be carefully choreographed, to avoid upsetting the French government. He wrote: 'The Tsarina told us later that the French Empress was very cheerful and charmingly sweet, but it was said she didn't return our visit because of a diplomatic difficulty and old age. And, in fact, after Cherbourg, they couldn't display their excellent relations – that would have displeased the republicans.'

Empress Eugenie may have decided, tactfully, not to return her visits; her advanced age, 83, might have been an additional obstacle. But the social whirl aboard *Thistle* continued unabated. The Empress's distinguished visitors included the Prince of Wales, Georgie and Earl Spencer, who enjoyed his encounter: 'Remembered me. Talked English – very old but with a charming manner'. Lord Suffield, another visitor, was equally taken with her unfailing good cheer: '[She was] telling me, as a great joke, of a cropper she had come on deck the day before, as if she had been 18 instead of about 80.' He himself was, or course, nearly 80.

❧

Nearly 2,000 miles away from the stultifying court in St Petersburg, the Romanov children were intent on enjoying themselves. The weather had grown sunny and the sea less menacing. They had all shaken off their seasickness and, having barely left the *Standart* for several weeks, the time had come to visit the pretty, leafy Osborne Bay, where their mother had played during her summer holidays.

During that last visit to Osborne, in 1894, Alix had written to Nicky ('bad Boysie') about visiting the bay and taking swimming lessons that had left her 'muchly frightened': 'How lovely the sea looked this evening when we sat out on the beach, all so peaceful and quiet, a real Sunday evening.' The letter concluded with one of her eerily prescient questions: 'Only this still, I love you, many more than words can express and daily my affection grows stronger and deeper – sweet, what will be the end?'

The children arrived at the public pontoon at East

Cowes, creating a minor security alert as they refused a motor car, insisting, instead, on two open horse carriages. They clearly had no worries about security for their short ride and were simply intent on enjoying a better view. Upon reaching the beach, they spent a merry hour collecting shells with their cousins, May, the Princess of Wales and Princess Mary, aged 12. May would have been happy to forego the *Britannia* cruise – she was not a keen sailor – and she loved the company: 'The children were delicious,' she wrote to her Aunt Augusta. In her diary she alluded to: 'the charming little Russian children, four girls and the boy'.

But the trip to the beach was not enough for the two eldest Grand Duchesses, Olga, now 13, and the newly-restored Tatiana. At two o'clock sharp, the girls were back at Trinity Wharf, all set for a shopping trip. They were not allowed to shop in St Petersburg, so it was with particular glee that they paid their halfpenny fare for the floating bridge to Cowes. This was an exciting taste of what the sheltered girls liked to call 'outside life'.

Their progress down the High Street was monitored by the Isle of Wight's stalwart Chief Constable, Captain H.G. Adams Connor, and his Deputy Chief Constable, Mr Gallaway. According to the *County Press*, the policemen 'kept the visitors under observation but did not make their official character known'. The girls wore discreet outfits, matching grey suits and straw hats, but were unable to tone down their high spirits. The reporter from the *County Press* was rather baffled by their enthusiasm: 'Their royal highnesses walked slowly through the main streets of Cowes, inspecting very commonplace shop windows with much eagerness and excitement.'

They were soon installed in the Beken Pharmacy. Ken Beken, whose grandfather Frank owned the shop, remembers being told about the young Grand Duchesses' visit. 'My grandfather said the royal party bought up most of his stock of hairbrushes and perfume. The girls said they were in short supply in Russia. They said it was nice to be in Cowes, where they were not being mobbed, but were treated with politeness and courtesy.' They bought postcards depicting members of various royal families, including their own adored parents.

Frank Beken was a keen photographer, and the young Grand Duchesses admired his photographs of sailing boats. What they presumably didn't know was that, during the review the night before, Beken had taken two photographs of the *Standart*. 'He said he was only just able to slip in between the circling picket boats, take a photograph and beat a hasty retreat, with one of them chasing him,' says his grandson.

At a second shop, the girls bought souvenirs of cufflinks and flags. They would present these, along with cigarettes, to favoured *Standart* officers, including Nikolai Sablin.

Further down the High Street, however, the girls fell victim to one of the 'mobbings' they so dreaded. They recognised fellow countrymen in a carriage drawn up outside the post office and cried out in Russian. One of the carriage party then produced a camera and the girls suddenly found themselves surrounded by a crowd. The *County Press* played it down: 'It is important to note that the temper of this large and miscellaneous assemblage was distinctly friendly and cordial, and the only rudeness exhibited was excessive admiration.

'The children themselves had not apparently been in the least frightened by the excited and rather closely pressing holiday crowd and they behaved with complete self-possession, smiling when one or two enthusiasts raised a cheer for them.'

But as excitement grew, several ladies pursued the girls into Benzies, the jewellers, and Captain Adams Connor was obliged to stand in the doorway to prevent what the *County Press* now admitted was 'troublesome homage'. It was Scotland Yard's Superintendent Quinn, the saviour of the choristers' blushes at Reval, who came to the rescue. He and the Metropolitan Police Commissioner, Sir Edward Henry, ordered police to line the street and clear a path for the royal party. If the girls earlier gave the impression they were enjoying themselves, their companions were less convincing. As the *County Press* reported: 'Some at least of their attendants were a little perturbed by the whole incident.'

A photograph exists of the girls and their trusty doctor, Eugene Botkin, in the High Street. All three look furtive and nervous. Olga is frowning and looking down at the ground, while trying to cram her left hand into her pocket, Tatiana looks nervously to her right, and fingers her top button. Botkin seems to be looking anxiously at Olga.

Dr. Botkin had only worked at court for a year, but he judged himself a cut above the other imperial doctor, Vladimir Derevenko, whom he denounced as 'of peasant stock'. At Cowes, he immediately made his mark, insisting Alexis be kept away from his 14-year-old cousin Prince Albert, 'Bertie' (later King George VI), who was laid low with whooping cough. The doctor was worried that fits of

Dr. Botkin with the two Grand Duchesses

coughing could trigger a haemorrhage in the little boy. How candid he was allowed to be about Alexis's illness is not known, but the result was that young Bertie, who should have played host to the children, was instead dispatched to Balmoral.

The courtly Botkin took the Tsarina's mysterious maladies seriously. Spiridovich was more sceptical; in his memoir he included a Russian professor's diagnosis of the Tsarina's ills: 'It was this illness, hysteron-neurasthenia, which had caused the Empress's exaggerated likes and dislikes, her bizarre way of thinking and acting, her religious exultation, her belief in the supernatural in general, and her faith in Rasputin in particular... The Empress's treatment was... entrusted to E.S. Botkin, who obeyed his patient in every way; he prescribed the treatment not as was necessary, but as the Empress demanded it.'

Botkin was equally smitten with the Tsar. When

Donald M. Wallace suggested to Botkin that the Tsar was 'fatalistic', Wallace recorded the doctor's retort: 'If fatalism meant a quiet trust in providence, he agreed.'

It was suggested to the Grand Duchesses that they move from the seething streets of West Cowes to Queen Victoria's Church, St Mildred's, at Whippingham. The Chief Constable ordered a landau for them and a wagon-ette for the team of police officers. But the girls, evidently fully recovered from their 'mobbing', refused to travel in the landau. In a repeat of the morning's dispute, they insisted on riding in the wagonette, so that they could see better.

On their way, they met Canon Clement Smith, who had been an honarary chaplain to Queen Victoria since 1893, remaining with her until her death. The Canon showed them around the church and the girls gazed at memorials put up by the royal family in memory of Queen Victoria. Their attention was caught by the Queen's surprisingly modest-looking blue chair. The Canon showed them the Battenberg Chapel, containing the tomb of the girls' uncle, Prince Henry of Battenberg, who had died of malaria, in 1896, shortly before the imperial family's visit to Balmoral.

'The young Grand Duchesses enjoyed their church visit and returned to the wharf at 5pm, laughing and talking...' reported the *County Press*.

During the afternoon, newspaper correspondents were invited on board the *Standart*, closely supervised by the first secretary of the Russian embassy and the ubiquitous Superintendent Quinn. The group was transported out, in style, on a steam boat attached to HMS *Excellent*, to be greeted by saluting sailors. The *County Press* lapped it all up, pronouncing the Russian Admiral Chagin 'the embodiment of courtesy and geniality'.

The journalists were shown round the Tsar's two studies and the grand dining room, before inspecting the Tsarina's private apartments, decorated with her favourite chintzes. In the drawing room, they spotted English books, including works by Shakespeare. The Tsar read regularly in English and would later while away many hours in captivity reading *A Short History of the English People*.

British naval officers and their wives were treated to champagne aboard several of the Russian boats. Spiridovich later admitted he was stumped by a request from one of the visitors: 'On one of our cruisers, the English asked for "Russian eau de cologne", although we are not sure why exactly.' Could the officers and their wives have been taken with Izvolsky's violet cologne? Or Dr. Botkin's? The doctor's scent was so distinctive that the young Grand Duchesses were able to trail him around the Alexander Palace, by following their noses.

Visitors to the *Polar Star* might well have come upon Izvolsky at his correspondence. It was on that day that he wrote another of his billets doux to Lady Savile, this time on beautifully annotated paper, headed with a picture of the *Polar Star*: 'Dear Lady Savile, best thanks for your two kind notes. I shall follow your directions and arrive at Newark on Saturday... It shall be such a pleasure to see you, yours sincerely Izvolsky.'

Some of the Russian sailors went ashore again, with those from the imperial yacht distinguished by the black and gold ribbons which adorned their caps.

Sablin revisited the High Street, glad to find all the shops now open; he wryly noted branches of grand Oxford

Street and Bond Street shops displaying luxuries: 'fatal for a wallet'. He registered a surfeit of 'marine items': 'for the ladies they were selling cushions with signal flags in very rich silk… brooches in the form of distinctive marine lanterns… bracelets with white enamel, in the form of life-buoys'. He also unearthed some first-class equipment for the *Standart*: 'mats for the boats, of excellent quality, white cable for the kayaks, small fenders for motor boats'.

⚜

The *Britannia* returned to the Cowes dock at 5.40, in good time for dinner, which was to be hosted by the imperial family on the *Standart*. The invitation specified that the dinner would take place 'a 8.30 heures le soir'. The Russian and British dates were both noted: '21 Juillet/3 Aout'.

In a letter to her ailing son Bertie, May, the Princess of Wales, pronounced the formidable *Standart*: 'a beautiful yacht and most comfortable'. The yacht had undergone a special overhaul for the royal dinner. Sablin found such preparations irksome, and he insisted the imperial couple shared his view: 'For the evening reception we turned the yacht into an unrecognisable salon, with the help of our artist, mechanical engineer N.N. Ulyanov. Throughout it, we hung electric bulbs hidden in multi-coloured light fabric, brought lots of flowers and arranged sofas on the quarter-deck. Their Majesties disliked that entire "masquerade" in the words of the Emperor.' The Tsar was, in fact, rather taken with the decoration: 'The quarterdeck was beautifully festooned with garlands.'

Sablin repeated the gripes he had originally expressed

at Reval: 'But that's why the life on the *Standart* was so different from that of *Victoria and Albert*. They [the British] had receptions and visits all the time and their entire yacht was decorated with carpets and flowers, while the *Standart* stood there like a great warship, with guards at the ramps and naval officers serving properly, as the Emperor loved it and demanded it to be that way.' Sablin would have deemed the informal efforts on the *Victoria and Albert* pointless, as, in his opinion, the British never quite mastered the art of 'hearty hospitality'.

❦

One guest, the Kaiser's German naval agent in St Petersburg, Captain Hinze, was generally viewed with suspicion. Sablin's opinion of him was, as usual, at odds with the others: 'He [Hinze] was the Kaiser's eyes and ears at the event. The British and our suite were unhappy with him being here. But Captain Hinze appeared to have a charming personality: very well-educated, secular, cheerful, helpful and one cannot say that he was an enemy of Russia – on the contrary, performing his duties, he always tried to soften them and enjoyed love and respect in Petersburg society as well as among us, the marine officers.'

The menu was impressive to the point of indigestibility: 'Potages Grand Veneur, Tortue Anglaise, Petite Patés, Truite Taymene, Homard et Moutarde, Longe de Veau Monglas, Filets de Canetons Bigarrade, Sauce Comberland, Punch Victoria, Roti-Dindonneaux et Brianneaux, Salade, Fonds d'Artichauts, sauce Ivoire et petits pois, Pêches Cardinal, Napolitaine glace, Dessert'. Georgie's and May's diary entries, however, were muted. 'Dined in full dress on board *Standart* with Nicky and Alicky, the whole family and suites,' wrote Georgie. His wife was equally sparing: 'David [the 15-year-old future Duke of Windsor] on board the *Standart* for dinner. The children appeared before dinner.' It was David, of course, who, as a toddler, had been deemed to have created a bond with the baby Olga at Balmoral.

The *Standart* boasted a strong musical contingent, travelling with a full brass band and balalaika orchestra. The *County Press* was enthusiastic: 'A Russian string band played during dinner and afterwards charming music was played by a special mandoline [sic] band.' The reticent May managed a compliment in her diary: 'The band played so well.' But Earl Spencer was intransigent: 'The crew played a Russian instrument sounding like a mandolin. Boys sang, Not very well. All the music so utterly sad.'

Wednesday 4th August
Georgie wrote in his diary: 'They came to Barton and had tea with us outdoors, their five delightful children came too.'

The third day was equally fine. 'It was everything that could have been desired, the sun shining brilliantly,' gushed the *County Press*. May agreed in her diary: 'Glorious day… sat out'. Georgie echoed his wife: 'A lovely day, nice breeze'. The Imperial family held a Te Deum to celebrate the birthday of the Dowager Empress Marie. The service was held in the *Standart*'s own ornate chapel.

Hours later, the choir boys were parading the streets of Cowes, dutifully waving Union Jacks. Presumably it was felt that they would be better employed waving flags than singing: Earl Spencer might have agreed. Cowes was still very much 'en fête' and the young Russian choristers would have mingled with professional entertainers, including itinerant musicians and 'strong men'. Among the prominent acts that year were a contortionist, Miss Nellie Scorey, and a Miss Dorothy Payn, judged 'mirth-provoking' by the *County Press* in her recital of 'The Winkle and the Pin'.

At some point, during that morning, contrary to earlier newspaper reports, rumours began to circulate that the Tsar would, after all, be coming ashore. As word spread that he was to visit Osborne in the early afternoon, boats began to gather around the bay.

It is not known exactly when the authorities finally agreed to allow the Tsar to land, but there was much deliberation over where he would take his momentous steps. 'The greatest precautions were taken to protect his royal person from the designs of undesirable persons,' reported the *Evening Post*. The decision was finally taken to hoodwink the public into believing that the Russian party would land at Trinity Pier, at East Cowes. The ploy involved the arrival of a fleet of smart motorcars carrying dignitaries including the commissioner, Sir Edward Henry, Superintendent Quinn and Admiral Fisher, who would doubtless have relished taking part in a scam. *The Straits Times* later disparagingly referred to: 'the well-organised scheme to keep the Tsar well away from visitors'.

By about 3.15, an expectant crowd had gathered at the pier and the *County Press* reported that: 'Everyone was on the tip-toe of expectancy'. Two police patrol boats steamed up the entrance to the River Medina, red flags flying at the bow. The patrol boats were followed by royal barges from the *Victoria and Albert* and the *Standart*. Excited spectators rushed to the gates of the wharf, only to watch as the procession sailed past. *The Straits Times* described the mood: 'Those who had cheers to give prepared to deliver them. The cheer was strangled at its birth. The gates were closed with a clang.'

When, 15 minutes later, they heard a royal salute, the crowd realised they had been duped. The Tsar had landed further up the coast. The landing stage at Kingston was selected because it was on private land. Henry Lucy was scathing about the subterfuge: 'After a long wait the crowd caught a glimpse of the royal barge, in which the Tsar was seated, as it swept past the pier, proceeding to an isolated spot to the eastward, where His Imperial Majesty hurriedly stepped ashore.'

If the Prince and Princess of Wales were aware of the ruse, they failed to mention it in their diaries. Georgie wrote breezily: 'All landed at Kingston up the river with N and A'. May was equally blasé: 'Went with parents to fetch Nicky and Alix and landed with at Kingston'. The Tsar either failed to notice the ploy, or thought nothing of it.

The bathos of the Tsar and Tsarina's return to Osborne was caught by *The Straits Times*: 'The car went up the leafy lanes... seen only by a handful of privileged observers and watchful men at crossroads wearing serge suits and yachting caps and trying their best not to look like policemen.' Henry Lucy wrote dismissively: 'He [the Tsar] visited England and left its shores without setting foot upon them, save in the way of a hasty, furtive visit to Osborne House. In connection therewith, the police precautions were ludicrous in their nicety.'

Lucy described how the beleaguered Tsar 'drove off at speed to Osborne House as if the furies were behind him'. *The Straits Times* described the car disappearing 'like a flash'. The King, characteristically unruffled, spent the drive chatting and smoking a cigar.

Those few lucky enough to spot the party would note that the Tsar, the King and the Prince of Wales were wearing matching yachting outfits: white topped caps, navy blue jackets, white drill trousers and white boots.

Back at Trinity Wharf, the thwarted crowd was rewarded with the appearance of the Romanov children, who climbed gaily into their car: 'A most happy and light-hearted little party they were, and they waved their hands and blew kisses in reply to the cheers,' reported *The Straits Times*. The *Evening Post* gave more details: 'There were the Grand Duchesses Olga, Tatiana, Maria and Anastasia, all in white, with puggaree veils round their soft straw hats.' In a reverse of paparazzi tradition, two or three of the camera-happy girls took snapshots through their car window. The reporter was particularly taken with the five-year-old Alexis: 'There was the Tsarevich in a white sailor suit, a chubby little fellow who is obviously the darling of his sisters. His podgy little attempts at a salute were the most amusing feature of the progress.'

Osborne House had ceased to be a royal residence after the death of Queen Victoria. By the time of the Tsar's visit, the estate had been converted into a naval college and convalescent home. The Tsar noted baldly in his diary: 'We looked over the newly constructed naval building, and then the palace of the deceased Queen where I had stayed 15 years ago – a sanitarium for officers was built there.'

The gates were closed an hour before the Tsar's arrival; police were stationed all round the inside and outside of the grounds. Earl Spencer had been an habitué of Osborne in its earlier days. He now found himself feeling nostalgic. 'I in the motor with the King, the Emperor, Baron Fredericks. Up to Osborne College… All looked so familiar.'

It was young David, the future Edward VIII, who greeted the cars at the main entrance, then showed the party the gymnasium and dormitories of the College. He was replacing his younger brother, Bertie, whose whooping cough had so worried Dr. Botkin. Georgie made a brief reference to his son: 'David arrived looking very well from Dartmouth.'

Years later David, by then Duke of Windsor, recalled: 'This was the one and only time I ever saw Tsar Nicholas. Because of the assassination plots, the imperial government would not risk their 'Little Father's' life in a great metropolis… I do remember being astonished at the elaborate police guard thrown around his every movement… This certainly made me glad I was not a Russian prince.' He had been further struck by the Tsarevich's 'large frightened eyes' when he had attempted to interest the little boy in the pattern of his school day. The Tsarina, he remembered, 'wore such a sad expression on her face'.

Following his jolly interlude with baby Olga at Balmoral, David had occasionally heard his grandmother, Queen Alexandra, saying that the young Grand Duchess would make a suitable bride for him. He decided now that he preferred Tatiana. He insisted that he was impressed by the way she tended her younger brother, Alexis, but it might also have helped that Tatiana was generally considered the prettier of the two.

The Romanov children enjoyed playing on the rolling lawns in the sunshine. Earl Spencer found the heat too much: 'The sun very hot'. He preferred to revisit haunts indoors: 'Looked at the room where we had sat with the Queen in '95 after dinner listening to a German officer playing the PF [pianoforte]'.

The Tsar and Tsarina visited the state apartments, which were unlocked specially for them. The Tsarina saw her beloved grandmother's deathbed, preserved exactly as it had been when she died. At the time, she had written to her sister, Victoria: 'I cannot really believe she has gone, that we shall never see her any more. England without the Queen seems impossible.' Donald M. Wallace recalled noticing: 'a tremor in the Tsarina's voice as she talked about the late Queen'.

She must have seen the portrait of her mother, Princess Alice, which still hangs on the wall of the dining room in which her parents were married. The portrait had been finished after her death from diphtheria, aged just 35, in 1878.

Before leaving Osborne for tea at the neighbouring Barton Manor, the Tsar signed the visitors' book with his customary flourish: 'Nicholas II Emperor of Russia'.

A Persian carpet had been laid outside Barton Manor and photographs were taken of the families. In one, the ten-year-old Maria leans against cousin Georgie, who has his arm around her. In another, Georgie rests his hands on the little Tsarevich's shoulders. In a third, Georgie and Nicky pose together, looking uncannily alike, both gazing intently at the camera. The Tsar leans towards the Prince, who puts his hand through his cousin's arm.

The shy young Tsarevich had resisted advances from the King and was not much more forthcoming with his cousin David. At Barton Manor, however, he came out of his shell, plying Sir Edward Henry's chauffeur with questions about the workings of the car. The party walked to the Swiss Cottage, which Nicky and Alix had visited in 1894. For the Tsarina, it would have been another poignant jolt from the past. Her mother, Princess Alice, and her siblings had once tended vegetables at the cottage, using miniature gardening implements; cooking had been accomplished on a tiny kitchen range.

While the imperial family was at Osborne, Sablin ventured further afield, to Portsmouth, where he found an unexpectedly hospitable consul offering a convivial 'Five o'clock' with 'a lot of pretty women'. Sadly, these particular members of what he called 'the beautiful half of the human race' could only speak English. 'Unfortunately, my English has always been bad and the British are very poor with foreign languages. So I spoke only with the consul, who knew French well.'

Georgie and Nicky with their sons

The English and Russian royal families at Barton Manor

Tea at Barton Manor

Izvolsky, meanwhile, received a journalist from Reuter's Press Agency on the *Polar Star*. Rising above his low spirits, he shrugged off the protests preceeding the Tsar's arrival, focussing, instead, on his fruitful talks with Edward Grey. The Tsar's visit, he insisted, was going very well.

He may have spoken too soon. The King and Tsar left Osborne at about 6.30; shortly after leaving, their car was forced to swerve, to avoid a private motorist. The monarchs reacted with surprising good humour: even the Tsar managed a smile. They were probably both relieved that their venture on to dry land was nearly over. Earl Spencer failed to mention the swerve at all, recounting only a subsequent difficulty on one of the yachts: 'Low water – so an inclined plain was all we had. The Queen was uneasy at it.'

On the last night, the parties were divided. The Tsar dined on the *Victoria and Albert* with the King, while the Tsarina entertained the Queen on the *Standart*. The Tsar gave only the barest details of his final evening: 'I went to the English yacht to a dinner for the members of the royal yacht squadron. I spoke for a long time with many people, and returned tired at 11.30 to our ship.' Georgie's entry was in the same vein: 'Papa gave a dinner on board to Nicky and members of royal yacht squadron… Sat down 38… bed at 12.' Like Earl Spencer on Monday night, he suffered with his feet: 'very tired after all the standing'.

Dining with the ladies on the *Standart*, Earl Spencer clearly felt himself banished to a sort of salon des refusés. He found his second Russian dinner no more appealing than the first, despite the best efforts of the chef. The French seems to contain some more obvious slips: 'Potage crème Princesse, consommé de volail [sic] aux quenelles, petits pates, Troncons de sterlet au Montrachet, Selle d'agneau de Pauillac printannier [sic], Parfait de foie gras aux truffes, Soyis au champagne, Roti-Poulardes du Mans et Gelinottes, Salade, Pointes d'asperge Sce. Mousseline Poires Duchesses, Comtesse Marie et bouchées, Dessert'. And the Tsarina was on poor form. As he wrote: 'Sat on left of the Empress. Not a good dinner. The Empress tired and less talkative. but told me several things about her life at home. She ate nothing but a few vegetables.' She brightened up solely when the subject shifted to their shared interest in outfits: 'She told me what she wore at the opening of the Duma.'

His concluding comments were unenthusiastic: 'Afterwards the same music... Got to my cabin at 11.50.'

May was, as ever, uncritical: 'I dined with Alix [Alicky] on *Standart*, nice little evening.'

Thursday 5th August

Georgie wrote in his diary: 'Nicky and Alicky gave large lunch on board *Standart* to which all family came. We cheered them. They go straight to Russia.'

The last morning was spectacularly fine. Georgie reported: 'Heavenly day very hot sun, practically a calm'. May echoed her husband: 'Glorious day... sat out', and Earl Spencer made a rueful note of the weather: 'Another very hot day'. The Earl successfully gained leave to go ashore, but found it unrewarding: 'Failed to get any photographs... mistook a launch, waited in the shade under a tree just behind club gardens. Pottered... in frock coat and yachting cap.'

The Tsar presented generous gifts to the various heads of security. Superintendent Quinn and Chief Constable Captain Adams Connor had helped, not least, with the rescue of the young Grand Duchesses from Cowes High Street. Both were now rewarded with gold cigarette cases with the imperial crest. Captain Adams Connor also received the Commander of the Order of St Stanislaus medal. A third officer involved in the girls' debacle, Deputy Chief Constable J.H. Galloway, was given gold and enamel sleeve links, set with sapphires and diamonds. Inspectors

Bignell and Salter received plainer gold sleeve links.

British sailors were awarded medals. On 16th August, Signalman Alfred H.E. Jenkins of HMS *Bellerophon* received an ornate letter from Buckingham Palace giving him permission to wear the Silver Medal of St Stanislas. The medal had been presented by 'His Imperial Majesty the Emperor of Russia' and the letter concluded with a flourish: 'I am, Sir, your obedient servant, Knollys'.

The Russian Admiral Chagin and Captain Nikolai Sablin were presented with gold mementos of Cowes, decorated with British and Russian flags; partly in compensation for not having been allowed to go ashore. Another member of the British party was given a silver cigarette case with a depiction of the British and Russian naval flags intertwined. On the back was carved: 'Alexandra Cowes 1909'.

The Tsar received deputations from the Corporation of the City of London, the Corporation of Portsmouth, the London Chamber of Commerce and the Liverpool Chamber of Commerce. In his diary, the Tsar reported receiving 'a beautiful small chest' from the department of commerce attached to the city of London. He presented £50 to the Royal Sailors' Home in Portsmouth for the creation of two cabins 'in the name of the Tsar and Tsarina'.

One thousand pounds (£80,000 in today's money) was set aside for the island poor. The mayor of Newport received a cheque for £400, accompanied by a letter from the Ambassador, Count Benckendorff: 'It is His Imperial Majesty's desire that this sum should be distributed amongst the poor of the Isle of Wight, excluding those of East and West Cowes, which have been provided for separately.'

The chairman of the Cowes and East District Council,

The silver cigarette case gifted by the Tsarina to a member of the British party

meanwhile, acknowledged its £600 share of the Tsar's gift: 'I am sure the two councils will distribute [the money] to the best advantage.' In fact, the gift created some bad feeling, as representatives of East Cowes became anxious about being short-changed. There were heated exchanges during a council meeting the following week. A conciliatory Mr A.E. Marvin Junior pointed out several reasons why the council should be grateful: 'His Imperial Majesty's visit last week attracted thousands of people to Cowes who would not otherwise have come there and it very largely contributed to Cowes having experienced one of the best regatta weeks that could be remembered for a long time.'

But the councillors of East Cowes were not so easily pacified: 'Mr Floyd said there was no doubt the population of East Cowes had greatly increased since the last census was taken. It was quite one third of that of Cowes and he thought East Cowes was entitled to at least £200 of the

£600.' Efforts were made to smooth troubled water: 'The chairman hoped there would be no unpleasantness over the question of apportionment.'

The Tsar's farewell message was unequivocal: 'The Emperor is deeply impressed by his visit to this country. The affectionate welcome accorded to him and the Empress by the royal family, the reception given by the magnificent naval force which saluted him at Cowes, the attitude of British statesmen, people and press are all happy auguries for the future. It is the Emperor's firm desire and belief that this all-too-brief visit can only bear the happiest fruit in promoting the friendliest feelings between the governments and people of the two countries.' Quoting the message, the *County Press* concluded: 'So may it be!'

He offered only the sparest account of the farewell lunch on the *Standart*: 'At 1pm the entire family and invited guests arrived for lunch. They wrote their names endlessly in books.' The *Standart* left sharply at 3.30pm, with bands playing and a salute of 21 guns. She was escorted, once more, by the three British destroyers, *Indomitable*, *Inflexible* and *Invincible*. The *Polar Star* followed, with the unfortunate cruiser, *Rurik*, over-compensating for her earlier difficulties. As the Tsar reported: 'The *Rurik* overtook us at full speed and stole away from us in order to sail around Skalen and Kiel.'

The King and Queen stood, with Georgie and May, on the forebridge of the *Victoria and Albert* to see them off. Thousands of spectators had gathered to watch the departure, but a haze soon engulfed the *Standart*. May wrote to her ailing son, Bertie: 'They left to our GREAT regret at 3pm.' The Romanovs, waving goodbye, were soon lost from sight.

By that evening the Tsar was thoroughly enjoying his respite from social pressures: 'The sea was ideal – completely still. After dinner I played a little at dominoes.'

May offered a cheery summing up of the visit to her son Bertie: 'Gone off very well. Both Uncle Nicky and Aunt Alix seemed to enjoy being here...' 'The visit was a great success,' she wrote to her Aunt Augusta on 6th August, 'and went off very well in every way. Both Nicky and Alix were charming and pleased to be here again.'

The *County Press* was exuberant: 'The rapprochement which has taken place between Britain and Russia is the most real contribution which has been made in our day to the cause of European peace and at the same time one of the most wonderful events that have marked the relations of powers to one another.' These sentiments were echoed in a journal in St Petersburg: 'No visit of the Tsar has ever been so full of significance as the one to Cowes and never have toasts proposed by chiefs of state been of such political import.'

Back at Tsarskoe Selo, the imperial family resumed their various routines. The Tsarina was laid low by the rigours of the trip, and shared her troubles, once again, with her long-suffering brother, Ernie. Her facial neuralgia was super-seded by a range of other symptoms, including her old leg pains: 'How I am paying for the fatigues of my visits, a week already in bed, as had such strong heart, back, leg aches and its [sic] a tiny bit better now, only sleepy pulse and very weak, strong anaemic [sic], lie all day. From 5 on get on my sopha [sic] – either on balconey [sic] or next room. After dinner N reads to me… I mostly lie with closed eyes, so tired, a little reading or looking at things gives headache, managed to sow [sic] a little yesterday – now my left kidney runs all over the place.' Three months later, she was still dwelling on her travails to a friend, in a letter written from the Crimea, in German: 'Ich bin recht krank wieder gewesen in Peterhof nach der Reise ins Ausland.' ('I've been really ill again in Peterhof following the trip abroad.')

Within weeks of their return, the Tsar had seen Rasputin at Peterhof. He wrote in his diary, 15th August: 'Went for a walk just before tea. Read until dinner. In the evening had a long talk with Grigory.' The Tsarina wrote to her husband from the Crimea: 'Sweet treasure mine, my huzy, dearly beloved one, God bless and keep you. G's [Grigory's] prayers watch over you on your journey, into his keeping I give you over.'

The girls had begun to share their most intimate secrets with Rasputin. In December, Olga wrote about a boy, called Nikolai, on whom she had developed a crush: 'My precious friend… It's hard without you: I have no one to turn to about my worries, and there are so very many of them. Here is my torment. Nikolai is driving me crazy. I only have to go to the Sophia Cathedral and I see him and could climb the wall, my whole body shakes… I kiss your hand. Your loving Olga.' Grigory advised an almost equally love-struck Maria, aged just ten, 'not to dwell on him'.

Through the early months of 1910, the imperial couple were seeing Rasputin every couple of days. The Tsar wrote in his diary on 27th January: 'After dinner I saw Grigory for half an hour'… On 3rd February: 'We talked for a long time with Grigory.' On 8th February: 'We saw Grigory.' On February 12: 'After dinner we saw Grigory.' On 14th February: 'I saw Grigory.' The following month the Tsar's sister, Xenia, wrote exasperatedly in her diary: 'He's always there, goes into the nursery, visits Olga and Tatiana while they are getting ready for bed, sits there talking to them and CARESSING them.'

The fragile new alliance between Russia and Britain would soon be rattled. With all the Tsar's talk, at the Isle of Wight, of 'happy auguries', the British remained distinctly unhappy about the political turmoil still plaguing the Romanovs in Russia. Georgie received intermittent news; his letter to Nicky, written in early 1910, sounds tentative and slightly condescending: 'I am glad to see that the Duma is getting on much better now and I hope in time that it will cease to give you trouble and anxiety.' Then, months later, on 6th May, King Edward VII died. Bertie, who had echoed his nephew with his allusions to 'the bonds that unite the people of our two countries', died surrounded by his wife; the Tsar's aunt, Alexandra; his daughter, Princess Victoria; and Mrs Keppel.

The Tsar sent an almost overly effusive letter to his cousin Georgie: 'I assure you that the sad death of your father has provoked throughout the whole of Russia a feeling of sincere grief and of warmest sympathy towards your people. God bless you, my dear old Georgie! My thoughts are always near you.' Georgie replied warmly: 'Yes, dearest Nicky, I hope we shall always continue our old friendship to one another, you know I never change and I have always been very fond of you.'

The cousins both paid tribute to the late King's efforts to create links between Britain and Russia. Georgie wrote: 'Yes indeed I know how, from the first, my dear father tried to do all he could to bring our two countries together and you may be sure that I shall show the same interest in Russia that he did.' Benckendorff remained unconvinced by the pronouncements of the new King and was so upset by Bertie's death that he had to go on leave. 'There is one thing a sovereign cannot bequeath to his successor – his personal prestige,' he wrote sorrowfully to a relation.

Other Russians shared Benckendorff's view, not least Stolypin, who had been so impressed by Bertie at Reval. But Stolypin would see only a few months of the new King's reign before being murdered, in a theatre in Kiev. Shortly after the murder, Lenin gave a talk, entitled 'Stolypin and the revolution' at the New Kings Hall, Commercial Road. The lecture marked Lenin's last visit to London.

The Russian Foreign Minister, Izvolsky, who had enjoyed such good relations with Bertie, soon had other preoccupations. On 10th October 1910, he wrote to Lady Savile from the Hotel Mirabeau in Paris: 'I got both your kind notes and I hope you received mine which I sent to Rufford Abbey. I intend to be in London (Hotel Ritz) on Friday next, and it will be such a pleasure to dine with you on Saturday and go to the play afterwards. I shall let you know as soon as I arrive in lond [sic]. Yours ever sincerely Izvolsky.'

Georgie and Nicky met, for one last time, in June 1913 at the wedding of the Kaiser's daughter Victoria. Nicky journeyed to Berlin by train, accompanied by 100 policemen. Georgie wrote a fond note in his diary: 'I had a long and satisfactory talk with dear Nicky, he was just the same as always.' The cousins' closeness remained a cause of consternation to the Kaiser, who was still convinced that they were plotting against him. 'William's ear was glued to the keyhole,' observed Georgie.

A year later, just before the outbreak of the First World War, the British Admiral, David Beatty, anchored on HMS *Lion*, at Kronstadt, alongside the *Standart*. The imperial family came on board for lunch. 'Never have I seen happier faces than those of the young Grand Duchesses, escorted over *Lion* by a band of middies especially told off for their amusement,' wrote the Ambassador Sir George Buchanan. 'When I think of them as I saw them that day, the tragic story of their deaths seems like some hideous nightmare.' By chance the imperial family were on board the *Standart* when the news came through that Franz Ferdinand had been murdered in Sarajevo.

The Russians and the British were allies during the Great War. But there were those at the Russian court who continued to harbour resentments. The Tsar's sister, Grand Duchess Olga, was convinced that, if the British had been less inept, the war could have been avoided altogether: 'If the British government had made it clear from the outset that England would join Russia and France if Germany made trouble, Willy would never have dared to make a single move. But I can tell you that Count Portales, Willy's Ambassador, told us in my own drawing room that he was convinced Britain would never enter the war.'

However, the alliance was fervently celebrated elsewhere. In December 1914, Mr Epps wrote a heartfelt letter of thanks to his former pupil, Olga, then 19, after she sent him a photograph of herself: 'As an Englishman the gift is, if possible, more acceptable at this time, when the Russian and English people are fighting together, as allies, against a common foe. Allow me to assure Your Imperial Highness that this gift will be treasured up for all time.'

During the first years of fighting, Georgie and Nicky exchanged a series of encouraging letters. On 27th December 1915, the King wrote from Buckingham Palace with news of yet another honour for the Tsar: 'I am anxious to appoint you a Field Marshal in my army as a mark of my affection for you...' Nicky replied from his military headquarters at Mogilev: 'I accept this distinction with much pleasure.'

On 5th June 1916, Nicky wrote: 'Everybody in Russia admires the magnificent way in which the English ships fought and tackled the whole German fleet in the North Sea [the Battle of Jutland]... My best love to dear May... God bless you, my dear Georgie... ever your most loving cousin and true friend, Nicky.' Georgie responded from Buckingham Palace: 'I am overjoyed at the splendid advance your gallant troops are making in Galicia and in your Western Provinces; it is wonderful the number of prisoners they have taken (nearly 300,000) and many guns and machine guns... Ever your most devoted cousin and true friend, Georgie'.

But Nicky's hold on power was slipping by the day, and revolution struck in March 1917. Civil unrest in St Petersburg could no longer be contained and the Tsar was persuaded by his advisers that he had no choice but to abdicate. Georgie sent a telegram on 6th March: 'Events of last week have deeply depressed me. My thoughts are constantly with you. And I shall always remain your true and devoted friend as you know I have been in the past.' It was never delivered. Later it emerged that the King had been obliged to reveal the telegram's content to the Prime Minister, Lloyd George. At a time when the new Provisional government in Russia was questioning the King's commitment to fighting the Germans it was judged too politically sensitive for Britain to be seen to be openly supporting the former Tsar; and the British embassy in St Petersburg was ordered to make sure it never reached the palace.

Objections had also been raised on the Russian side, with the Foreign Minister insisting that the telegram would be misinterpreted as part of a ruse to help the Romanovs escape.

At that early stage, the King did certainly appear to be broadly behind the idea of the deposed Tsar and his family seeking refuge in Britain. He wrote in his diary, on 10th March: 'Went over to Marlborough House and had a talk with mother dear [Queen Alexandra, who was also, of course, the Tsar's aunt] about Russia and Nicky; she is very much upset about it all.' The next day he wrote: 'Michael [the Russian Grand Duke Michael Mikhailovich] came and we discussed the idea of poor Nicky coming to England.'

The British government issued a formal offer of asylum towards the end of March, and there was a period when the Romanovs could have left Russia and come to Britain. The Tsar's nephew, Prince Dmitri, certainly believed that the new provisional government would have been happy to let them go, writing in an unpublished memoir: 'Alexander Kerensky [the provisional government leader] was willing to allow them to leave and in fact keen that they should. A British cruiser was standing ready at Murmansk, but at the last minute Lloyd George decided against the evacuation.'

In fact, in the end, it was not Lloyd George but the Tsar's 'true friend' and dear cousin, Georgie, who took the fateful decision. The King had fallen under the influence of his jittery private secretary, Lord Stamfordham, becoming increasingly anxious about a growing republican movement. In his former incarnation as Sir Arthur Bigge, it had been Stamfordham, who had been so put out by the 'Russian occupation' of Balmoral in 1896. Now, in 1917, he took it upon himself to keep the deposed Tsar at bay, judging him a threat to the stability of the British nation.

When Lloyd George suggested the King put a house at the imperial family's disposal, Stamfordham replied stiffly that the only available place was Balmoral: 'which would not be a suitable residence at this time of year'.

On 30th March, Stamfordham wrote to the Foreign Secretary, Arthur Balfour: 'The King has been thinking much about the government's proposal that the Emperor Nicholas and his family should come to England. As you are doubtless aware, the King has a strong personal friendship for the Emperor and therefore would be glad to do anything to help him in this crisis. But His Majesty cannot help doubting, not only on account of the dangers of the voyage, but on general grounds of expediency, whether it is advisable that the imperial family should take up their residence in this country.'

The Foreign Secretary, Arthur Balfour, at this point opposed Stamfordham, writing: 'His Majesty's ministers quite realise the difficulties to which you refer in your letter, but they do not think, unless the position changes, that it is now possible to withdraw the invitation which has been sent, and they therefore trust that the King will consent to adhere to the original invitation, which was sent on the advice of His Majesty's ministers.'

But Stamfordham was not backing down. On 6th April he wrote another letter to Balfour: 'Every day the King is becoming more concerned about the question of the Emperor and Empress coming to this country. His Majesty receives letters from all classes in life, known or unknown to him, saying how much the matter is being discussed, not only in clubs, but by working men, and that Labour members in the House of Commons are expressing adverse opinions to the proposal.

'As you know, from the first the King [Nicky's cousin, Georgie] has thought the presence of the imperial family (especially of the Empress) in this country would raise all sorts of difficulties and I feel sure that you appreciate how awkward it will be for our royal family who are closely connected with the Emperor and the Empress....

'The King desires me to ask you whether, after consulting the Prime Minister [Lloyd George], Sir George Buchanan [the Ambassador in Russia] should not be communicated with, with a view to approaching the Russian government to make some other plan for the future residence of Their Imperial Majesties?'

That same evening, Stamfordham wrote with even greater urgency: 'He [the King] must beg you to represent to the Prime Minister that, from all he hears and reads in the press, the residence in this country of the ex Emperor and Empress would be strongly resented by the public and would undoubtedly compromise the position of the King and Queen. Buchanan ought to be instructed to tell Miliukov [Russian's Foreign Minister] that the opposition to the Emperor and Empress coming here is so strong that we must be allowed to withdraw from the consent previously given to the Russian government's proposal.'

Under this continuing barrage, Balfour began to falter, sending a minute to Lloyd George: 'I think the King IS placed in an awkward position.

'If the Tsar is to come here we are bound publicly to state that WE (the government) have invited him – and to add (for our own protection) that we did so on the initiative of the Russian government (who will not like it).

'I still think that we may have to suggest Spain or the south of France as a more suitable residence than England for the Tsar.'

Four days later, Stamfordham ratcheted up his campaign with a visit to Lloyd George at Downing Street. Balfour finally agreed to send a telegram to Buchanan, informing him that their previous agreement, to admit the Tsar, was no longer binding.

The King was becoming increasingly paranoid, fearing for his popularity, even for his throne. The possibility that public opposition to the Tsar might result in some kind of uprising was not so remote. Republican rallies had been held at the Albert Hall and demonstrations had taken place in industrial centres, including Glasgow and Liverpool. There would be a major incident, months later, in February 1918, during which 3,000 soldiers marched on Whitehall.

Then there was the issue of finance. How much would it cost to keep the Romanovs in suitable grandeur? This is now regarded as one of the central stumbling blocks. In the end, some believe that all these discussions of a British welcome were purely academic. The historian Robert Service is adamant that radical left-wing members of the provisional government would never have allowed the Romanovs to leave Russia.

In the summer of 1917, when Buchanan told the provisional government leader, Alexander Kerensky, that the British government had withdrawn its offer, the imperial family were under house arrest at Tsarskoe Selo. Kerensky never forgot Buchanan's discomfort: 'With tears in his eyes, [he was] scarcely able to control his emotions.' Within weeks, the imperial family had been taken from St Petersburg to their Siberian exile in Tobolsk.

By now the Tsar's trust in the British was waning fast. Aside from the withdrawal of their invitation, there was an outlandish belief, at court, that Buchanan had conspired against the Tsar with several hostile Romanov cousins.

The imperial children's English tutor, Sydney Gibbes, had followed the family to Tobolsk in October. 'He [the Tsar] absolutely pounced on me at first, for it was from English sources that he had received the severest blows,' wrote Gibbes 'Attacks from revolutionary leaders in Russia he knew he must take and suffer, but those from England – to which he had been so loyal – had to be the unkindest cut of all.'

On the day when the Bolsheviks finally seized power, Nicky noted in his diary that he sawed wood and underwent a consultation with his dentist. With all his dread of dental work, Nicky seems to have had his dentist with him in Tobolsk. He read details of the events in St Petersburg some weeks later. Gibbes described his shocked reaction: 'I had never seen the Emperor so shaken. For the moment he was completely incapable of saying or doing anything, nobody dared to say a word.'

Two months later, in December 1917, Gibbes took the unusual step of writing a letter to the Tsarina's former governess, Madgie, in London. In the letter, he gave a description of the location of the house in Tobolsk, including a sketch of the layout of the interior. At one point, he referred to David, the future Duke of Windsor, who had played with the baby Olga at Balmoral and who, aged 15, had shown the imperial family around Osborne College: 'I hear that David is back from France, how are his father and mother? And the cousins, are they also at the front?'

This letter was addressed to Miss Margaret Jackson at a Home for Governesses in Regents Park. It was clearly written with the intention of aiding some rescue attempt by the British. As Gibbes later said: 'The Empress was sure that Miss Jackson would carry the letter to the Queen.'

Eighteen months later, Gibbes, then in Vladivostock, wrote to an unnamed British official wanting to know what had happened to the letter. There was evidence of its having reached St Petersburg, but nothing further.

To assist the Romanovs' efforts to adapt themselves to their life in captivity, Mr Gibbes came up with the idea of staging obscure one-act plays in Russian, French and English. During a performance of the English playwright Harry Grattan's *Packing Up*, the youngest Grand Duchess, Anastasia, created some welcome hilarity when she mischievously lifted her skirt to reveal her father's Jaeger underwear.

In February 1918, the Bolsheviks phased out the Russian Julian calendar, forcing citizens to adopt the Western Gregorian calendar. The Tsar felt he had simply lost 13 days; he railed in his diary: '18 January or Feb 1 (new time). There'll be no end to misunderstandings and confusion.' There was little mention of cousin Georgie during this period, though his name was raised when the Bolshevik guards discussed the removal of 'citizen Nicholas Romanov's' epaulettes. Fearing that the Tsar would resist, one of the more lenient guards warned there would be consequences if King George V heard that there had been some sort of struggle. But the Tsar dealt with the issue peaceably, agreeing to wear a short black coat when walking outside. Henceforth, he would wear his military tunic only when he was inside.

Towards the end of April 1918, the Tsar and Tsarina were told they must leave Tobolsk. The British government had not issued another formal invitation, nor had they instigated any serious rescue attempt. But it seems that, at this point, the imperial couple were still living in hope that they would end up living in Britain. That, at least, was what they told their faithful Dr. Botkin, who had accompanied the family to Tobolsk. The doctor passed the reassuring news on to his teenage children: the Tsar, he said, would attend a show trial in Moscow, after which the imperial family would be exiled to Britain.

The Tsarina's sister, Victoria, harboured hopes of getting the female members of the imperial family to England at the very least. In May 1918 she wrote to the Foreign Secretary, Arthur Balfour, begging him to allow the Tsarina and her four nieces to live with her on the Isle of Wight. Writing from Kent House, she pointed out that, though Alexis might be a 'political asset', the women could be 'of no value or importance as hostages to the Russian government.' Balfour replied that the Foreign Office couldn't trust the Bolshevik government to do any kind of deal, adding that any such plan could be construed as a Tsarist conspiracy. But he gave a forlorn promise to look for other opportunities.

The Bolsheviks' decision to move the imperial family from Tobolsk was beset by difficulties as it became clear that the Tsarevich Alexis was too ill to travel. It was eventually decided that the Tsar and Tsarina would form an advance party, taking only the 18-year-old Grand Duchess Maria and Dr. Botkin with them. The doctor assured his children they would soon be reunited in England. He told his son he must spend a year there, before entering the Academy of Theology. The young Botkins eagerly assembled their father's belongings in a trunk. His son Gleb, then aged 18, was struck by the strangeness of packing tennis flannels and white tennis shoes amidst the snowy wastes of Siberia.

As it turned out, the party was transferred to Ekaterinburg, in the Urals. The rest of the imperial family joined the Tsar, Tsarina and Maria in May. Two months later, on the night of 16th-17th July, all seven members of the imperial family were murdered in a cellar along with Dr. Botkin. The murder took a full 20 minutes to complete as bullets ricocheted off the jewels they had sewn into their clothes for safekeeping.

Days after the killings, the English tutor, Mr Gibbes, managed to get into the house. He pocketed various keepsakes, including several of the Tsarevich's bloody bandages. He later combined these macabre keepsakes with a pair of the Tsar's felt boots that he had brought from Tobolsk. A tattered notebook was found in a filthy washroom, behind some pipes. It bore the inscription: 'For my own beloved Nicky to put to good use when he is far away from his Spitzbube. From his love Alix, Osborne, July 1894.'

When news began to circulate in Britain that the Tsar had been murdered, Georgie must have been horrified. A memorial was organised at the Russian Church in London for 'dear Nicky'. But Stamfordham tried to prevent the King from attending, insisting that the news of the Tsar's death had yet to be official confirmed: 'Public opinion is in a hypersensitive condition and might misconstrue anything done by the King into sympathy with the counter-revolution in Russia. Meanwhile, it seems to me we could decline to join in the G. Duchess George's service on the grounds that the government have no official news of the Emperor's death.' Georgie may not have fully expressed his sorrow, still less any contrition, but he did defy Stamfordham with his decision to attend the memorial. On 25th July he wrote in his diary: 'May and I attended a service at the Russian Church in Welbeck Street in memory of dear Nicky, who I fear was shot last month by the Bolshevists. We can get no details. It was a foul murder. I was devoted to Nicky, who was the kindest of men and a thorough gentleman: loved his country and people.'

A month later he wrote of the fate of the rest of the imperial family: 'I hear from Russia that there is every probability that Alicky and four daughters and little boy were murdered at the same time as Nicky. It's too horrible and shows what fiends these Bolshevists are. For poor Alicky, perhaps it was best so. But those poor innocent children!'

The King now made desperate attempts to rescue his aunt, the Tsar's mother, who was by then in the Crimea. She was finally persuaded to leave, in April 1919, on a British battleship, HMS *Marlborough*, with 16 other Romanovs, including her daughter, the Tsar's sister, Grand Duchess Xenia, and five of Xenia's sons. The party was accompanied by six dogs and a canary.

Most of the 17 Romanovs were taken to Malta. After several days, they boarded a second British ship, the *Lord Nelson*, for England. It was the crew of the *Lord Nelson* who had been photographed cheering the King and the Tsar at Cowes ten years before.

King George's reunion with his surviving cousins took place at London's Victoria station. One of the Russian servants fell to her knees in front of the King, having mistaken him for the cousin he so resembled. A friend of the Tsar's nephew, Vassily, said the family never forgot that moment: 'It was embarrassing for the Dowager Empress and Xenia. Vassily found it excruciating.'

IN 1998, JUST OVER A HUNDRED YEARS after the imperial visit to Balmoral, the Royal Scots Greys, now known as the Royal Scots Dragoon Guards, escorted five members of the imperial family to their final resting place. The bodies of the Tsar, Tsarina, Olga, Tatiana and Anastasia, exhumed in the Urals, at the start of the decade, were borne into the Peter Paul Fortress, in St Petersburg, to the accompaniment of pipes and drums.

As for the various other characters involved in the Romanovs' sad story, Madgie, Miss Margaret Jackson, died at her Home for Governesses in Regents Park, in January 1918, just a month after Mr Gibbes posted his letter from Tobolsk. She was 82 and had been in a steep decline mentally and physically, so would have been unable to help in any kind of rescue effort.

Margaretta Eager died in 1936, aged 72, at the Grange Nursing Home, in Keynsham, Bristol. Her Holland Park boarding house had not proven a success, but she left a full £218. She was very insistent that her niece should not benefit from her death: 'I leave NOTHING to my niece

Frances Macleod because I spent nearly £400 on her education, travelling expenses and clothes.'

The English tutor, Mr Epps, had returned to England, following his dismissal, in 1908. In February 1918, he delivered a talk about his experiences in Russia to the Church of England Men's Society, in Yorkshire. Belying his reputation as a gossip, Epps made no mention of the imperial family, focusing instead on the chaos of revolution. The 'miseries of life without discipline were sufficiently illustrated', reported the *Harrogate Advertiser* drily. Epps died, aged 87, in 1935. His nephew subsequently sent 31 treasured papers to Maggs, the antiquarian book dealers for pricing. The papers, including colourful drawings by the little Grand Duchesses, were then forgotten, languishing in a drawer for nearly 70 years before being restored to the Epps family in Australia.

Following the murders of the imperial family, the tutor, Mr Gibbes, travelled from Siberia to Manchuria, where he was ordained a Russian priest, changing his name to Father Nicholas, after the Tsar. He returned to England in 1937 and subsequently established a Russian orthodox church in Oxford. At every service, he commemorated the Tsar, Tsarina, Tsarevich and four Grand Duchesses. In his chapel he stored a chandelier that had hung in one of the imperial family's rooms in Ekaterinburg and the Tsar's felt boots from Tobolsk. He died in 1963, in St Pancras' hospital, London.

❧

Of those Russians involved in the Anglo-Russian 'entente',

several survived the revolution. The moody *Standart* officer, Nikolai Sablin, was arrested twice before escaping to Romania, where he joined groups struggling against communism. He ended his days in a Romanian prison, dying of heart failure in 1962. General Alexander Spiridovich, the Tsar's head of security, was arrested and imprisoned, but then unexpectedly released. He and his family settled in Paris, where he worked as a historian. He died in 1952.

Sablin's namesake, the *Standart*'s Captain Nikolai Sablin, became the Tsar's aide-de-camp but refused to accompany the family to Siberia. The Tsarina was said to have been particularly upset by this and other demonstrations of disloyalty from *Standart* officers. The Captain did, however, fight for the White Army, before leaving Russia in 1920. He died in Paris in 1937.

The anglophile Russian Ambassador, Count Benckendorff, died, in January 1917, two months before the first revolution. The Foreign Minister, Alexander Izvolsky, died in Biarritz, in 1919.

The slippery double agent, Evno Azev, took refuge in a Balkan monastery, having been condemned to death by Prince Kropotkin, Burtsev and the other revolutionaries. He later fled to Germany, where he died, aged 49, in 1918.

The principal British dignitaries who had attended the meetings were not directly affected by the revolution. The Ambassador in Russia, Arthur Nicolson, was succeeded by George Buchanan in 1910 and died in 1928. The 6th Earl Charles Spencer, who made such an effort at the Isle of

Wight, died in 1922, aged 64, after contracting a chill at a public event in Northamptonshire.

The Russian radicals, Prince Kropotkin and Vladimir Burtsev, both lived to see the revolution. The Prince set off from Bromley to St Petersburg, just days after the Tsar's abdication, proclaiming: 'What they reproached us with as a fantastic utopia has been accomplished without a single casualty.' He arrived at the station in the early hours of the morning, to be greeted by a crowd of 60,000.

Kropotkin successfully gave advice to Kerensky throughout the summer of 1917, but then fell out with Lenin, comparing his policies to those of the 'darkest middle ages'. He died, aged 78, in 1921. His funeral marked the last meeting of the Russian anarchists: their persecution, by Lenin's secret police, the Cheka, began days later.

Vladimir Burtsev also ended up opposing Lenin, protesting that the Bolsheviks were acting for the Germans and that they were agents of the Kaiser. On the day of the October Revolution, Trotsky had Burtsev arrested; he came to be seen by some as the first political prisoner of the USSR. He was freed, months later, subsequently living in exile in Finland, Sweden and finally France. He died in Paris, impoverished, in 1942, aged 79.

Of the grand spectators at Cowes, in 1909, the names of at least two would be forever linked to the Romanovs. *The*

New York Times's biggest spender, Nonie May Leeds, would have glimpsed the youngest Romanov daughter, Anastasia, on the *Standart*. What Nonie could not have known was that, after her death, in 1923, her young son, Billy, would play host to the false Anastasia at the Leeds' sumptuous house on Long Island. Billy's wife believed the mentally unstable Anna Anderson to be the real Anastasia, and the claimant would live with the Leedses for several months before Billy decided he'd had enough and threw her out, along with her two parakeets. The Anastasia debacle was said to have cost Billy Leeds his marriage.

One of Nonie May Leeds's guests on her floating palace *Margareta*, Lady Muriel Paget, set up a hospital in St Petersburg six years after the Isle of Wight meeting. The Anglo-Russian hospital was based in the palace of Grand Duke Dmitri Romanov. And when, in 1916, Grand Duke Dmitri conspired with Prince Felix Yusupov to murder Rasputin, the hospital provided a refuge for Yusupov, who checked himself in, claiming to have choked on a fish bone.

The Cowes pharmacist, Frank Beken, whose shop proved such a hit with the two young Grand Duchesses, became established as a marine photographer. Three years after the Romanovs' visit, he captured a picture of the *Titanic* setting off on her first and last voyage. Frank Beken died in 1970. His grandson, Ken Beken, now runs the Beken and Son marine photography business. He has a picture of the *Titanic* on the wall, alongside his grandfather's hard-won photograph of the *Standart*.

The *Standart* herself was stripped down after the revolution, before being pressed into military service. She was renamed plain *18 Marta* (18th of March), then just *Marti* and served as a minelayer during the Second World War before being damaged in an air attack at Kronstadt. She was renamed *Oka* in 1957, then scrapped at her old haunt, Tallinn (Reval), in 1963. King George V's yacht, *Britannia*, was sunk in the Solent upon his death, in 1936. The *Victoria and Albert* was scrapped in 1955.

⚜

And what of the lavish gifts? In February 2017, one of the Tsarina's presents for her twin godchildren in Harrogate was put up for sale at Bulstrodes, the auctioneers, in Dorset. The boxed set of Fabergé cutlery was expected to fetch £10,000. It fetched £20,000.

The nephrite vase set with cabochon moonstones and chalcedony, presented to Bertie by Nicky at Reval, is now in the Royal Collection. The Wilkinson sword given, in turn, to Nicky by Bertie, is in the museum at Tsarskoe Selo. With the sword is a Scots Greys Uniform, presented, in April 2017, by a group of retired officers of the Royal Scots Dragoon Guards. The presentation of the uniform, conducted by a Brigadier Melville Jameson, marked the first official visit by the former Scots Greys for 122 years.

A chain presented by Queen Victoria to Nicky is now on show at one of the Kremlin Museums in Moscow. The chain should have been returned to the British royal family, but Queen Elizabeth II allowed it to stay in Russia. According to the museum director, Yelena Gargarina, '[Queen Elizabeth] wrote a wonderful letter saying that she wanted as many people in Russia as possible to see this chain and to recall the tragic story that occurred to a member of her family 100 years ago.' Several members of the Romanov family have been to see the chain, some intimating that they might make some kind of claim for it. Yelena Gargarina, the daughter of the spaceman Yuri Gargarin, dismisses them outright, insisting that they are no different from the 2.2 million other visitors to the museum and that they are 'just tourists'.

The Tsar's sister, Grand Duchess Xenia, was one of the few Romanovs to settle in Britain. More or less penniless and destitute, Xenia readily accepted cousin Georgie's offer of a house on the Frogmore estate, at Windsor, where Nicky and Alix had stayed during their engagement. In 1925, the Grand Duchess moved into Frogmore Cottage, along with a sizeable family contingent.

These Romanovs had very little to do with their royal neighbours. Xenia's grandson, Prince Andrew Romanoff, remembered just one tea at the castle with the Queen, or 'Auntie Mary' as he was instructed to call her. The King never registered the young Prince. He once spotted the boy bowing and doffing his cap as he swept past the family's garden gate in a royal car. He later rang to ask who 'the little gentleman' was.

On one occasion Xenia's grandchildren created a furore when they tucked into three enormous Easter eggs intended for the little Princesses Elizabeth and Margaret: the packages had been wrongly delivered. Another time, Prince Andrew was cycling through the Windsor Castle Grounds when he met the young Princess Elizabeth. He greeted the future

Queen, three years his junior, with an elaborate: 'How do you do?' That evening Xenia received a phone call saying her grandchildren were not to walk in the private gardens while the British royal family was staying at the castle.

Georgie's general avoidance of the poor relations did not extend to the Grand Duchess herself. She was regularly entertained at Buckingham Palace, with her son, Prince Dmitri, accompanying her to dinners.

The King took pains to avoid all blame for the deaths of the imperial family. Dmitri later wrote: 'I twice heard King George refer to Lloyd George as "that murderer" in the presence of my mother.'

In 1933 Georgie seems to have had no compunction about buying the Tsarina's Fabergé mosaic egg at half cost, for £250, from Cameo Corner in London. It had been given by the Tsar to his wife in 1914 and contained portraits of all five children. The legendarily acquisitive May was the lucky recipient.

It took decades for the full story to emerge about the role played by the palace in refusing sanctuary to the Romanovs. Two key memoirs were written before the King's death, in January 1936: in both he escaped any blame. The Ambassador, George Buchanan, insisted, in 1923, that the invitation had never been withdrawn; his daughter's claim, nine years later, that he had falsified his account to protect the King, as well as his Foreign Office pension, made little impact.

In 1934, Lloyd George diplomatically rewrote the relevant chapter of his *War Memoirs*. The later, published version made no mention of the King, or Stamfordham: 'An agitation had also started in this country, which indicated that there was a strong feeling in extensive working class circles, hostile to the Tsar coming to Britain,' he wrote. 'However, the invitation was not withdrawn. The ultimate issue in the matter was decided by the action of the Russian government, which continued to place obstacles in the way of the Tsar's departure.'

Thirty years on, in his global bestseller, *Nicholas and Alexandra* (1968), Robert K. Massie summarised the King's directive in a way that suggested a measure of cool pragmatism: 'Because of the outburst of public opinion, the Russian government should perhaps be informed that Britain was obliged to withdraw its offer.' Massie admitted, however, that after the murders: 'memories tend to blur'.

Three years later, in 1971, Earl Mountbatten, the son of the Tsarina's sister Victoria, continued to blame Lloyd George, rather than the King, breezily telling an interviewer: 'Oh yes, in the early days he discussed it with my mother, he was very anxious to offer them asylum over here, but the government, the Prime Minister, Lloyd George, was understandably opposed on political grounds at the time of the war and I think it would have been very difficult therefore to go against him.'

The matter was finally laid to rest in 1983, with the publication of Kenneth Rose's biography of George V. Here, the woeful correspondence between Stamfordham and Balfour was quoted in full. There is no ambiguity in Rose's chilling conclusion: 'The King's volte-face was complete. With the concurrence of his ministers, he had ensured that, whatever else might happen to his Russian cousins, they should not set foot in England. The original offer of asylum, to which both sovereign and Prime Minister had subscribed, was a dead letter.'

When Rose asked the Queen for permission to print the papers, she had gamely responded: 'Let him publish.' The Queen Mother had not been so equable, dropping Rose from her lunch party list. Her private secretary told Rose: 'Your chances of an MVO [Member of the Victorian Order] have just floated out to 50 to 1.'

The controversial Tsarina may have played a large part in the King's decision. The British royal family were worried about her German roots and what they saw as her mental instability. The historian Hugo Vickers refers mutedly to the 'strain in nerves of the Hesse-Darmstadt family line, inherited in full by the Tsarina'. The unimaginative King may well have been haunted by the social implications of having his cousins in Britain, worried that his life would be subsumed in awkward social situations, a never-ending imperial tea party.

There is a memorial to the imperial family on the Isle of Wight, in Queen Victoria's church, St Mildred's of Whippingham. It is curiously hard to find. The plaque is modestly sized and almost hidden, on an inside wall of the Battenberg chapel, which is itself usually locked. Those who succeed in finding the memorial, may read the names and birth dates of the members of the imperial family who 'perished in the Russian Revolution on the 17th July 1918', among them Olga and Tatiana, who, as two carefree young girls, paid a visit to the church on that hot summer after-noon of 3rd August 1909.

BIBLIOGRAPHY

Aronson Theo: Grandmama of Europe, The Crowned Descendants of Queen Victoria (London, John Murray, 1972)

Botkin, Gleb: The Real Romanovs (New York, Fleming H Revell, 1931)

Brook-Shepherd, Gordon: Uncle of Europe (London Collins, 1975)

Butterworth, Alex: The World That Never Was (London, The Bodley Head, 2010)

Buxhoeveden, Baroness Sophie: The Life and Tragedy of Alexandra Feodorovna: Empress of Russia (London, Longman, 1928)

Carter, Miranda: The Three Emperors (London, Penguin, 2009)

Clark, Ronald W.: Lenin: The Man Behind The Mask (London, Bloomsbury Press, 2011)

Clarke, William: The Lost Fortunes of the Tsars (Stroud, Gloucestershire, Sutton Publishing, 1994)

Cowles, Virginia: Edward VII And His Circle (London, Hamish Hamilton, 1956)

Duff, David: Queen Victorian's Highland Journals, edited by David Duff (Hamlyn, London, 1997)

Edwardes Anne: Matriarch Queen Mary and The House of Windsor (London, Hodder and Stoughton, 1984)

Erickson, Carolly: Alexandra: The Last Tsarina: The Tragic Story of the Last Empress of Russia (New York, St Martin's Griffin, 2001)

Fisher, J.A.F.: Fear God and Dread Nought Correspondence Vol 2 (London, Jonathan Cape, 1956)

Grey, E.G.: Twenty-Five Years 1892-1916 (London, Hodder And Stoughton, 1925)

Hardinge, Charles, Baron: Old Diplomacy; The Reminiscences of Lord Hardinge of Penshurst (London, J.Murray, 1947)

Hibbert, Christopher: Queen Victoria in her Letters and Journals (Gloucestershire, Sutton Publishing, 1984)

Hough, Richard: Edward and Alexandra (Sevenoaks, Kent, Hodder and Stoughton, 1992)

HRH The Duke of Windsor: A King's Story (Prion, 1998)

Izvolsky, Alexander: Au Service de la Russie – Correspondance Diplomatique 1906 – 1911 Vol 1 (Paris, 1937)

King, Greg: The Last Empress (London, Aurum Press Ltd, 1994)

King Greg: Twilight of Splendour: The Court of Queen Victoria During Her Diamond Jubilee Year (Hoboken, New Jersey, John Wiley, 2007)

Lee, Sir Sidney: King Edward VII, A Biography Vol II: The Reign (London, Macmillan and Co Limited, 1927)

Lucy, Sir Henry William: Diary of a Journalist, Volume 2, 1890 – 1914 (London, John Murray, 1921)

Magnus, Philip: King Edward the Seventh (London, John Murray, 1964)

Mallet, Victor: Life With Queen Victoria: Marie Mallet's Letters from Court, 1887-1901, edited by Victor Mallet (London, John Murray, 1968)

Massie, Robert K.: Nicholas and Alexandra (New York, Atheneum, 1967)

Maylunas Andrei andMironenko Sergei: A Lifelong Passion (London, Weidenfeld and Nicolson, 1996)

Morris, Jan: Fisher's Face (London, Viking, 1995)

Plumptre, George: Edward VII (London, Pavilion, 1995)

Ponsonby, Sir Frederick: Recollection of Three Reigns (London, Odhams Press)

Nicolson, Harold: Sir Arthur Nicolson, First Lord Carnock, A Study in the Old Diplomacy (Constable and Co, London, 1930)

Radzinsky, Edvard: The Last Tsar: The Life and Death of Nicholas II (London, Hodder and Stoughton, 1992)

Rappaport, Helen: Four Sisters (London, Macmillan, 2014)

Ridley, Jane: Bertie: A Life of Edward VII (London, Vintage Books, 2012)

Rounding, Virginia: Alix and Nicky, The Passion of the Last Tsar and Tsarina (New York St Martin's Press, 2012)

Sablin, Nikolai: Ten Years on the Imperial Yacht *Standart* (in Russian) (Russia, Petronius, 2009)

Service, Robert: The Last of the Tsars, Nicholas II and the Russian Revolution (London, Macmillan, 2017)

Soroka Marina: Britain, Russia and the Road to the First World War (Farnham, Surrey, Ashgate Publishing Ltd, 2011)

Spiridovich, General Alexander: Last Years of the Court at Tsarskoe Selo Vol 1 (Fremantle, Western Australia, Russiahouse Press, 2009)

Suffield, Lord: My Memories, 1830 – 1913 (London, Herbert Jenkins, 1913)

Summers Anthony and Mangold Tom: The File on the Tsar (London, Victor Gollancz, 1976)

Tisdall, E.E.P.: The Dowager Empress (London, Stanley Paul and Co Ltd, 1957)

Trewin J.C.: Tutor to the Tsarevich (London, Macmillan, 1975)

Van de Kiste, John: Crowns In A Changing World: The British and European Monarchies 1901-36 (Stroud, Gloucestershire, Sutton Publishing, 1993)

Vovk, Justin C.: Four Royal Women, The Fall Of The Age Of Empires (Bloomington, Indiana, iUniverse, 2012)

Wilson A.N.: Victoria: A Life (London, Atlantic Books, 2013)

Yusupov, Felix: Lost Splendour (London, Jonathan Cape, 1953)

Zeepvat, Charlotte: From Cradle to Crown (Stroud, Sutton Publishing, 2006)

Other sources

The Diaries of Emperor Nicholas II 1906 – 1909 Volume III Part A: Translated, Edited and Annotated by Stephen R de Angelis, PhD. Powered by Bookemon, Sunnyvale California, 2011.

Louisa Lady in Waiting: The personal diaries and albums of Louisa, Lady in Waiting to Queen Victoria and Queen Alexandra, compiled and edited by Elizabeth Longford (London, Jonathan Cape 1979)

Unpublished diary of the 6th Earl Charles Spencer, property of the present Earl Spencer

Unpublished memoir of Prince Dmitri Romanov, property of his granddaughter, Penny Galitzine.

National Archive, Kew

Country Life, August 2, 1984

Isle of Wight County Press

Isle of Wight Evening Post

Isle of Wight Times

The Isle of Wight Times and Hampshire Gazette

The Isle of Wight Observer

Majesty Magazine

Straits Times

European Royal History Journal: Royalty on the Isle of Wight, by Sue Woolmans. November-December, 1998.

Russians in London, Sarah J Young

Imperial Russian Journal, Volume 5, Number 3: The 1896 Balmoral Visit To Queen Victoria of Emperor Nicholas II and Empress Alexandra by Julia P Gelardi, 2001

New York Times, June 10 1908

Romanov News, no 117, December 2017, and no 106, January 2016, edited by Ludmila and Paul Kulikovsky

Romanoff, Andrew: The Boy Who Would Be Tsar: The Art of Prince Andrew Romanoff. A book published to accompany an exhibition of the artwork of Andrew Romanoff, organised by Griff Williams and presented by Gallery 16, San Francisco, 2007.

ROYAL ARCHIVE SOURCES

Quotations used with the permission of Her Majesty
Queen Elizabeth II.

Balmoral

Alix: 'Fondest thanks dear letter Nicky agrees to all' RA VIC/
MAIN/H/47/63

Alix: 'Nicky and Alicky much distressed' RA VIC/MAIN/I I/
47/87

Victoria complaining of 'great inconvenience' RA VIC/MAIN/H/
47/77

Carington: 'arrangements exactly the same' RA VIC/MAIN/H/47/78

Chief Constable's Office: 'Tuesday and 22nd erased and, mysteriously
'RA VIC/MAIN/H/47/83

Carington: 'Russian Embassy says Tsar wants to land' RA VIC/
MAIN/H/47/67

Carington: (Prince of Wales) 'deprecating changing Leith for North
Queen's Ferry' RA VIC/MAIN/H/47/68

Carington: 'I conclude he will be sent to Siberia' RA VIC/
MAIN/H/47/74

Carington: 'I was constrained to tell him' (the Naval Attache) RA
VIC/MAIN/H/47/82

Carington: (Luggage) 'We have received no answer' RA VIC/
MAIN/H/47/74

Alix: 'so happy meeting soon' RA VIC/MAIN/H/47/87

Sir Francis Knollys: 'take care to acquaint the Emperor that it will be
warm' RA VIC/MAIN/H/47/50

Metropolitan Police Report: '3 Russian Detective officers now residing
with... Head Gardener' RA VIC/MAIN/H/4//88

Carington: 'two persons who are to live in the artists rooms at Balmoral are Russian police' RA VIC/MAIN/H/47/54

Sir Edward Bradford: 'The Emperor is safer here' RA VIC/MAIN/H/47/86

Robert Anderson: 'the practical danger which was serious and urgent is now happily at an end' RA VIC/MAIN/H/47/69

Sir Matthew Ridley: 'I do not believe that this plot had anything to do with the Tsar's visit' RA VIC/MAIN/H/47/76

Robert Anderson: 'makes me glad that the Tsar is there' RA VIC/MAIN/H/47/92

Maldolm Delavigne: 'Three officers will remain during visit' RA VIC/MAIN/H/47/79

Carington: 'all well weather still rainy' RA VIC/MAIN/H/47

Victoria: 'I think you could not do otherwise now' RA VFIC/MAIN/H/47/59

Russian national colours RA VIC/MAIN/H/47/75

Carington: 'volunteer will line the whole route from Leith Port' RA VIC/MAIN/H/47/74

Levee dress will be worn RA VIC/MAIN/H/47/85

(train) departed sharply (from Ferryhill Junction) at 5.50 RA VIC/MAIN/H/47/85

Inspector Baxter: 'gloves and leggings will be worn' RA VIC/MAIN/H/47/83

May: 'a true highland welcome' RA QM/PRIV/CC24/18

Nicholas O'Connor: 'I gather that the Emperor is looking forward' RA VIC/MAIN/H/47/45

Lord Salisbury's aide: 'a minimum temperature' RA VIC/MAIN/H/47/73

Georgie: 'they were charmed by their visit' RA GV/PRIV/AA12/51

Reval

Inspector General of the Forces: 'let me know the approximate dates on which the King will leave for and return' RA PPTO/PP/EVII/MAIN/C/26220

Alexander Izvolsky: Dress Frock Coat RA PPTO/PP/EVII/MAIN/C/26220

Hugh O'Beirne: 'The promise has not been kept' RA PPTO/PP/EVII/MAIN/C/26220

Colonel Arthur Davidson: 'anything like a wholesale distribution NEVER takes place' RA PPTO/PP/EVII/MAIN/C/26220

Commodore of the *Victoria and Albert*: 'counting on two police inspectors coming' RA PPTO/PP/EVII/MAIN/C/26220 enamelled spoons for Mrs Knollys RA FandV/VISOV/1908:Reval

Isle of Wight

Herbert Gladstone: 'Mr Keir Hardie spoke' RA VIC/MAIN/R/30/60

'The King CANNOT agree' RA VIC/MAIN/R/39/60

Herbert Gladstone: 'in using the word 'restraint'' RA VIC/MAIN/R/39/62

Herbert Asquith: 'an incitement to the assassination of the Tsar' RA VIC/MAIN/R/30/21

Edward Grey: 'It is I fear impossible to make any impression upon the extreme men' RA VIC/MAIN/W/55/50

Resolution of Protest RA PPTO/PP/QV/ADD/PP3/39

Admiral Konstantine Nilov: 'general indifference to Russian Navy' RA VIC/MAIN/W55/53

Georgie's diary: 'read and rested as I was pretty tired' RA GV/PRIV/GVD/1909: Aug

May's diary: 'the anchor of St Catherine' RA QM/PRIV/QMD/1909

Georgie's diary: 'beautiful night but rather cold' RA GV/PRIV/GVD/1909

Georgie's dairy: 'there was a fair breeze' RA GV/PRIVE/GVD/1909

fatalism of Tsar RA VIC/MAIN/W/55/53

May's letter to son Bertie: 'a beautiful yacht' RA GVI/PRIV/RF/11/040

Georgie's diary: 'lovely day, nice breeze' RA/GV/PRIV/GVD/1909

Georgie's diary: 'drove in motors' RA GV/PRIV/GVD/1909: Aug

Georgie's diary: 'Heavenly day' RA GV/PRIV/GVD/1909: Aug

May's letter to son Bertie: 'left to our GREAT regret' RA GVI/PRIV/RF 11/040

May's letter to Aunt Augusta: 'Nicky and Alix were charming and pleased to be here' RA QM/PRIV/CC25/39

Acknowledgements

Thanks to Charles Spencer, who supplied me with the diaries of the 6th Earl Spencer; Michael Hunter, who showed me round Osborne House and sent cuttings; Dawn and Alex Haig-Thomas, who showed me round Barton Manor; Simon Dear from the Isle of Wight Record Office; Hugo Vickers, who spoke to me about Lord Stamfordham and the Tsarina; Robert Harris, who gave me further information about the Romanovs' visit to Paris in 1896; Ian Shapiro, who provided photographs, papers and a cigarette case given to a member of the British party by the Tsarina; Charles Gibbes, who allowed me access to Sydney Gibbes' diaries; the indefatigable Sue Woolmans, who tracked down various papers, including the relevant entries from the Tsar's diaries; Janet Epps who shared her knowledge of her relation, the tutor John Epps; Maggs Bros, the antiquarian book dealers, who supplied papers about Mr Epps; Carol Graves-Johnston, for introducing me to the work of Prince Andrew Romanoff; Alan Marriott, Editor of the Isle of Wight County Press; Ken Beken of Beken of Cowes Marine Photography; Robert Golden; Anne Springman; Alan Champion; John Groves and Jim Green; Miranda Carter, who came up with the idea; Nicholas Underhill, who read early drafts and offered plenty of good advice; Aurea Carpenter, friendliest and most meticulous of editors; and, of course, my family, Craig, Tallulah and Silas.

INDEX

Frances Welch is the author of *Rasputin: A Short Life* (2014), *The Russian Court at Sea* (2011), *A Romanov Fantasy* (2008) and *The Romanovs & Mr Gibbes* (2004), all published by Short Books. Frances Welch has written for the *Sunday Telegraph*, *Granta*, *The Spectator* and the *Financial Times*. She lives in Aldeburgh, Suffolk, with her husband, Craig Brown. They have two children.